Oliver —
I know Randal
liked you to have, had

from
Judy

RANDALL SWINGLER

SELECTED POEMS

RANDALL SWINGLER

Selected Poems

Edited, with an introduction and notes, by Andy Croft

TRENT EDITIONS

Published by Trent Editions 2000

Trent Editions
Department of English and Media Studies
The Nottingham Trent University
Clifton Lane
Nottingham NG11 8NS

© The Swingler Estate 2000

All rights reserved. No part of this book
may be reproduced in any form, except by
a newspaper or magazine reviewer who wishes
to quote brief passages in connection
with a review.

Printed in Great Britain by Goaters, Nottingham
ISBN 1 84233014 4

Contents

Introduction and acknowledgements · vii
Further Reading · xxi

THE YEARS OF ANGER

I Premonitions 1936-38

Summer Beauty	3
Return to Reality	5
Bruern Wood	6
Elegy	7
In the Silence	8
Fear	8
The June Larks	9
Acres of Power	10
As Christmas Wanes	12
The Prisoner	12
The Possible	14
Praise for the Anonymous	15
After May Day	16

II The Ordeal of Love 1936-40

Letter I	17
Letter II	18
Letter III	19
Letter IV	20
Letter V	21
Letter VI	22
Letter VII	22

III Farewell 1937-40

Envoi	24
Sussex in Winter	25
Sad Evening	26
Strange Fields	27
Interim	27
The Fighter is Calm	28
March, 1939	29
August Bank Holiday, 1939	30
The Beginning of War	33
Testament of an Army of Fatalists	34

IV Battle 1943-45

The Exiles	36
Briefing for Invasion	37
Heavy Shelling at Night	39
No Second Front this Year	40
The Line that divides the World	41
Infantry coming out of the Line	42
For What Crime?	43
The Gothic Line	44
Between Agony and Desire	46
The Day the War ended ...	48
No Pity, No Poetry	49

The God in the Cave

Lazarus or The Walking Dead

Sonnet 1	53
Sonnet 2	53
Sonnet 3	54
Sonnet 4	54
Sonnet 5	55
Sonnet 6	55
Sonnet 7	56
Sonnet 8	56
Sonnet 9	57
10 Ending	57

11 Beginning	58	Advance Democracy	76
		Ballad of Heroes	77
Reflections on the Walls of a Palaeolithic Cave		On Some Who Were Killed Fighting in the International Brigade	78
1 Incantation	59	Make Your Meaning Clear	80
2 The Cave-artist's Prayer	59	Sixty Cubic Feet	81
3 Myth	60	Drinking Song	82
4 Landscape	60	Z Reserve	83
5 The Inner Darkness	61	Return to a Battlefield	84
6 Puritan Childhood	61	The Winter Journey	86
7 Church	62	My Mistress Played	88
8 Resurrection	62	To Geraldine	89
		Millie's Song	90
Uncollected Poems		Chorus	91
Song of the Hunger Marchers	65	London Nocturne	91
Before Morning	66	Three Trees	92
Man Like Sun	66	In the Labyrinth	92
Especially When I Take Pen in Hand	67	The Ballad of Herod Templer	93
		Your Train has Gone	94
from Entrance to the City	68	The Harvest of Peace:	
from Spain	69	A Cantata	95
They Live	70	A Rose for Lidice	103
Friends, We Would Speak a Little of This Performance	71	*from* The Fall of Babylon	103
		Carol	104
Triumphal Song for the Peacemaker	74	Peasant Philosophy	105
		These Were the Dove Days	106
After the Pogrom and the Stench of Blood	75	Aspen, Apple, Ash	106
		One Dark Bird Wandering	107
Notes	108		

Introduction

Randall Swingler is the missing lyric poet of the 1930s and 1940s. No English writer worked harder to mobilise public opinion in the name of Peace, or fought more bravely to prosecute the World War when it could no longer be avoided. He was responsible for some of the most imaginative interventions of the Popular Front years, and he wrote some of the finest poetry of the Second World War. A playwright, novelist, critic and poet, he edited six literary magazines, and his verse was set to music by many of the most distinguished composers of his generation.

Although they do not contain all his best poems, *The Years of Anger* (1946) and *The God in the Cave* (1950) are nevertheless Swingler's two most important books. Published between the end of the Second World War and the start of the Cold War, they provide an extraordinary and unique record of the middle years of the century, from the romantic Communism of the early thirties, through the campaigns of the Popular Front and the years of anti-Fascist War, to victory in 1945 and the subsequent disappointments and betrayals of Cold War Europe.

Swingler was born in 1909. His father was assistant curate at Aldershot Parish Church, later vicar of Long Eaton in Nottingham and Cranbrook in the Weald of Kent. One grandfather was a Derby iron-master, railway-builder, coal-owner and Deputy Lieutenant of Derbyshire. The other was a Colonel in the Seaforth Highlanders and the Madras Artillery, advisor to the Maharaja of Mysore and personally responsible for the brutal suppression of the Indian Mutiny in Raipore. His uncle and godfather was Randall Davidson, the Archbishop of Canterbury. Church, Army, Empire, iron and steel, railways and mines, represented at Westminster and at Court – this was an extraordinary concentration of wealth, power and influence, a remarkable inheritance, even by the standards of the Edwardian upper-middle classes.

Swingler was educated at home until he was ten, followed by preparatory school in Sussex and an Exhibition to Winchester. There he gained a reputation as a scholar, runner, flautist, poet and a reforming head of house; among his admirers at school were Richard Crossman and Thomas Hodgkin. In 1928 Swingler went to New College, Oxford to read *Literae*

Humaniores. He won a running Blue and joined the University Climbing Club. He played in the Oxford Orchestral Society and the Oxford Opera Club Orchestra, and for a while considered a career as professional flautist. Friends included Peter Burra, Louis MacNeice, Gabriel Carritt, and the composer John Sykes. He joined the Promethean Society and the Oxford Group, wrote religious verse-plays for a local Boys Club and poems for the undergraduate magazine *Farrago*.

After a brief religious crisis, Swingler failed 'Greats' and left Oxford to teach in a preparatory school in London. In 1933 he married the concert pianist Geraldine Peppin, for whom he wrote *Poems* (1932). Living in London, Swingler began to examine the society in which he enjoyed such a privileged position and to question the social purposes of poetry. His second collection, *Reconstruction* (1933) was an emotional and political response to London, and a renunciation of the Georgian landscapes of his early poetry. Reconstructing himself as a poet of the modern city, Swingler exchanged the influence of Robert Bridges for the manifesto manner of Auden, a brief experiment that produced the widely acclaimed *Difficult Morning* (1933).

In 1934 Swingler joined the Communist Party – via Lawrence, Blake and the New Testament – and like the Young Man of Great Possessions, immediately donated most of his inherited wealth to the Party. Through the Communist Party he met other young radical writers and artists with whom he was to work over the next twenty years, notably Edgell Rickword, Montagu Slater, James Boswell, Jack Lindsay and Alan Bush. As an editor, speaker, organiser, journalist, critic, playwright, poet, novelist and publisher, Randall Swingler was one of the leading figures in the cultural life of the Communist Party, in turn the organising centre of the Popular Front campaigns to mobilise London literary life against Fascism and war. He was active in the St Pancras Branch of the Communist Party and in the Party's Ralph Fox Writers Group. He was involved in the Workers Music Association and the Left Book Club, especially the Poets Group and the London Writers and Readers Group. He was an editor of the magazine *Left Review*, where he published Nancy Cunard's *Authors Take Sides on the Spanish War*, and by the end of the decade was the literary editor of the *Daily Worker*. In 1937 Chatto and Windus published his first novel, *No Escape*. He wrote a new version of *Peer Gynt* for the Group Theatre (where he was assistant editor of the *Group Theatre Magazine*) and he wrote several plays for Unity Theatre, including the Mass Declamation *Spain*, the Munich-play *Crisis* and revues like *Sandbag Follies* and *Get Cracking*. In 1938 he launched his own radical paperback publishing company, Fore Publications, selling half a million of the Key Books series in the first twelve months. He and Alan Bush wrote *Peace and Prosperity* for the London Choral Union, and co-operated on a radically re-written production of Handel's *Belshazzar* for the London Co-operative Movement. Together they edited the *Left Song Book* for the Left Book Club, and in 1939 they organised the Festival of Music and the People, including an Albert Hall pageant written by Swingler and starring Paul Robeson, and the premier of Britten's *Ballad of Heroes*, for which Swingler and Auden provided the libretto. His second novel, *To Town* was published in 1939.

Although Swingler was privately opposed to the British Communist Party's characterisation of the War (following instructions from Moscow) as an 'imperialist' conflict which it was the duty of Communists to resist, he publicly supported the new line, writing a series of anti-war songs with Alan Bush, and organising the cultural activities of the anti-war People's Convention. He took over the editorship of the magazine *Poetry and the People*, re-launching it as the anti-war magazine *Our Time*, and became a staff reporter for the *Daily Worker,* writing anti-government Blitz journalism until the paper was banned in 1941.

After the German invasion of the Soviet Union the Communist Party declared its support for the War and Swingler brought the magazine *Seven* into the Fore Pubs stable as a magazine of writing from the Forces. Called up at the end of 1941, Swingler spent seven months at Catterick Camp, training as a wireless operator. In September 1942 he sailed with the 56th Divisional Signals to India and Iraq, where they were to support the Red Army in the Caucasus. When it was clear that the German drive south had stopped at Stalingrad, they travelled through Palestine and Egypt to Libya, joining the Eighth Army at Enfidaville and the last battle for Africa. A few months later, in September 1943, the Allied invasion of Italy began at Salerno. Swingler was in one of the first parties ashore, and was in almost continuous action for the next twenty months, up through the mud of Italy to Gradisca on the Yugoslav border. He took part in heavy fighting on the Volturno and Garigliano rivers, at Monte Camino, on the Anzio beach-head, at Casteltorte, on the Germanno and Coriano ridges, at Rimini, on the Senio Bulge and the River Po. For his part in the battle of Lake Commachio, Corporal Swingler was awarded the Military Medal for bravery.

The Years of Anger

Swingler was out of uniform and back in London by March 1946. He was physically and spiritually shattered, suffering from alapecia and insomnia, drinking heavily and temporarily estranged from Geraldine. Tormented by the memory of what he had seen and done during World War Two, he was nevertheless missing its comradeship and purpose. Post-war London was a dispiriting place, and to returning servicemen it seemed both ruined and unchanged by six years of war. But on Communist Party pub-crawls across Soho Swingler began to make a slow and partial rehabilitation, and by the end of the year he had recovered sufficiently to start collecting the poems he had brought back from Italy, together with some of his unpublished verse from the 1930s.

The last time Swingler had tried to put together a collection, at the beginning of the war, he had included all his best-known propaganda pieces. This time, however, he selected a sequence of highly personal lyric poems, distinguished by a sensitivity to English landscape and literary tradition, less concerned with historical events than with the impact of history on individuals. This does not mean that *The Years of Anger* is somehow politically muted (although the *Daily Worker* did not know what to make of it), rather that Swingler's Communism reached well beyond the vocabulary of mere 'politics'. 'I think it is important to add that these are the poems of a Communist,' he wrote, 'because it is often supposed that considerations of personal and poetic development are sacrificed as soon as the freely consented discipline of that party is undertaken, whereas I believe that Communism is the only fully creative attitude to life in our day, the only fully poetical attitude to life.'

The Years of Anger draws on work written over the previous decade, including poems first published in *Caravel*, the *Daily Worker*, *Left Review*, *Life and Letters Today*, the *London Mercury*, *New Writing*, *Our Time*, *Poetry and the People* and *Twentieth Century Verse*, and in war-time anthologies like *Rhyme and Reason*, *New Lyrical Ballads* and an anthology edited by Oscar Williams, *The War Poets* (1945). Swingler wrote of his collection:

> These poems were all written during a period of ten years, from 1935 to 1945, a period during which I was totally absorbed in thought and action by the struggle first to prevent the World War which seemed inevitable; and second, to create a system of social organisation which would render such wars unnecessary and unthinkable. If they have any interest or value, it rests in the chart of inner development which they provide of someone implicated, as we all were in our varying degrees of consciousness, in the stress of those years. Poetry of this character is often more honest and more revealing than reasoned statement, because it arises, even against the reluctance of the conscious mind to admit its formulations, from the deepest levels of human reaction to

events, and the pattern which results is often surprising and bewildering to the writer himself. I believe that it is essential that we should understand the changes which history, and our action in it, have wrought in us, and that possibly such poems as these can help us to do so .... They represent the efforts of one individual creatively to cope with the huge and brutal circumstances of history, to "subject the inner forces to his own control," and to achieve that personal freedom which is the recognition, and understanding, of necessity. (Epilogue to *The Years of Anger*)

The selection allows the poems to tread in each other's footsteps, tripping over the same imagery of Summer and Winter, the personal geography of each poem an overlapping fragment of a larger map of the times. The earliest poems in the first section, 'Premonitions 1936-38' establish the book's emotional landscape, detailing the loveliness of the English countryside with an unaffected simplicity at the same time as they try to resist its temptations. In the mid 1930s the Swinglers had lived in a cottage in the Cotswolds; their daughter Judith was born there in 1935. After the outbreak of the War in Spain, they returned to London in order to be closer to 'the middle of the conflict.' The poems thus examine the collision between private happiness and public helplessness, identifying private, sexual and domesticated contentment with a paralysing inertia and the 'idiocy of rural life'. The later poems in this section aspire to control and unify all aspects of living, to break down barriers within and between individuals, and between the individual and society. They seek to Anglicise their revolutionary content by invoking a deepened sense of belonging to an older, native, radical tradition.

The second section, 'The Ordeal of Love 1936-41', consists of a series of letters in verse addressed to Geraldine, still trying to reconcile love and revolution, beauty and politics, private joy and public anger. The country-and-city debate is here expressed as the choice between love and politics. Between one round of meetings, rehearsals, performances and the next, the Swinglers did not always see very much of each other. But he was also preparing himself and Geraldine for the war he knew must come, and which he did not expect to survive. The third section, 'Farewell 1937-40' is thus a combined valediction to the English countryside and to the settled, early years of their marriage and the possibilities of ordinary living in an age of crisis.

The war-poems are the unavoidable climax of the book, as the war itself was the consequence of the failure to prevent it. The eleven poems in the final section, 'Battle', tell the story of the longest and bloodiest campaign in the West, recorded, uniquely, from the point of view of the ordinary soldier, in uniform, on the move, in the front line, all the way up through the mud of Italy to VE Day. Influenced by the poetry he had been able to read during the campaign – Aragon, Vercors, Euripides and Homer – the poems also drew on Edward Thomas, John Cornford and the Nonesuch *Blake* which he had carried with him ('the old boy and I are such peculiar old friends and understand each other. He keeps the world big and interesting and important'). There is a Homeric quality to the writing, celebrating the brutal masculinity of the common fighting man, but acknowledging the shared suffering and the loss of personality required to fight a necessary war; asserting the genuinely heroic nature of the war to liberate Europe but testifying to the degradation of human values which it demanded:

> I go back to Yeats' remark that 'out of our quarrel with the world we make rhetoric', political slogans, mass declamations or whatnot and 'out of our quarrel with ourselves, poetry'. The point is that the war was not like a storm descending suddenly on us, it was a fate which we wove for ourselves, in the making of which every one of us had a hand, and consequently the real underlying conflicts of it were not simple, as they were for the Red Army man. The development of that conflict of ours was the most important thing in the war, was something arising out of the internal contradiction of our nature, and what was needed, what they were all looking for when they cried out for War Poets, was an illumination of that inner war and the outcome of which alone will illumine the character of this post-war world and life. The fighting soldier, I think, mostly worked out in practice the solution of his inner conflict, if he solved it. If he didn't, he perished – deserted, fell in the bag, went mad, or 'got his'. But just because of the terrific complex of contradictions which made up his position he was forced to solve his own problem for himself (why he was fighting, should he fight, what and how to fight) for his life's sake. The story of this war then, from the fighting soldier's viewpoint, does not lie in a description of experiences, of what he 'went through'. That was all done in the last war by Owen and Sassoon … in that other war it was an experience which was negative, it oughtn't to be happening, had to be stopped. In this war it had to go on, to the end, and the protest against it, though a real element in the internal conflict, was not the whole thing. But writers in this war have been misled into following Owen and Sassoon, who really were protesting against the objective horrors of their experience, whose conflict was an external one against the conditions of the world. The story of this war for the British people

is the story of 'why' we did what we did, the story of our developing consciousness through struggle, not only 'what' the soldier experienced, but 'how' he felt and what he did with the experience. The story of the last war was the story of man's fate and how it mastered him: the story of this war's the story of our fate and how 'we' mastered it. (Letter to Geraldine Swingler, 11 November 1945)

The Years of Anger was published by Jack Lindsay's Meridian Books just before Christmas 1946. It should have sealed Swingler's reputation as an unflinching witness to his time and generation, a link between the romantic Communism of the early 1930s and the anti-Fascist victory of 1945. But as Swingler feared, literary London was now dominated by writers like Spender, Connolly, Eliot, Lehmann and Orwell, who had spent the war a long way from any fighting: 'Isn't it odd that scarcely anyone contributing to any of these anthologies and magazines is actually in the fighting forces? How do they manage to keep out? If anyone wants to know why writing hasn't taken much of a step forwards lately that's the answer I think. They've missed the crucial experience of our time.' As the combatant's verse began to appear in print over the next few years, it was too late. London critics were already bored by World War Two. As early as April 1946 Spender was arguing in *Horizon* that there 'were no war poets' and that poets must anyway resist the pressure to respond to 'an age of overwhelming public events'. Later that year in *Poetry Since 1939*, Spender suggested that, although the war may have 'stimulated much indiscriminate writing and publishing of poetry' among men and women serving in the Forces, 'the best poems written were by older men and women whom the war effort almost passed over' – that is, by writers like Stephen Spender. In July, John Lehmann was urging contributors to *Penguin New Writing* to turn away from writing about the war and to write instead about experiences of a 'more wider and more generally valid scope'. London literary culture had survived World War Two intact. *The Years of Anger* was barely reviewed.

The God in the Cave
By 1947 Swingler had begun writing again for the *Daily Worker*. He was editing *Our Time* with Edgell Rickword, writing songs with Alan Bush, writing and presenting programmes for the BBC, and teaching part-time in adult education for the University of London. He had an affair with the novelist Penelope Dimont; their daughter, Deborah, was born the following year. Everything Swingler had touched – poetry, politics and love – had hitherto turned to gold. From now on, everything – especially poetry,

politics and love – seemed to turn to ashes and ruin in his hands. As the Cold War set in, Swingler found himself attacked from both sides. He was denounced by Orwell, criticised inside the Communist Party for 'liberal' sympathies and purged from both the BBC and adult education by the gathering anti-Communist witch-hunt. After a series of rows with the Communist Party over the direction of *Our Time*, the magazine folded in 1949. He and Jack Lindsay launched another magazine, *Arena*, under the slogan, 'European, with no Iron Curtain', thus guaranteeing the hostility of both the book-trade and the Communist Party (which ordered them to turn it into a 'fighting journal of Socialist Realism'). In desperation, Swingler founded yet another literary magazine in 1950, with John Davenport and Paul Hogarth. When their backer discovered that his editors were Communists, he withdrew his support and *Circus* closed after only three issues.

The God in the Cave was published a few months later as part of Fore Publications' ambitious Key Poets series (which also included George Barker and Edith Sitwell). The first half of the book consisted of a terrifying sonnet sequence in which Swingler cast himself as Lazarus, or 'the Walking Dead.' The sonnets draw on his experiences at Monte Camino in 1943, when his signals unit was hit by enemy shelling and buried alive. Swingler was exhumed, after two and a half hours, to find he was the only survivor. He was unhurt, but the full horror of this incident stayed with him for the rest of his life, shaping his imagination with a morbid hunger for the darkness of the grave, weighing him down with overwhelming feelings of guilt that he should have survived when so many had perished. Soon after he was de-mobbed Swingler went to see Harry Pollitt (General Secretary of the Communist Party), hoping that Pollitt could use his influence to find him a job as a miner. He wanted to recapture the dangerous and intense *elan* he had enjoyed among the ordinary ranks in the Signals; but it also looks like a craving to return to the source of his horror, the expression of a death-wish.

> ... when a man expects to die, and doesn't, he strips himself naked as he never before knew himself to be and leaves all his coverings behind. So that when he emerges on the other side, he feels unprotected and ashamed as if everything that death should have done has been exposed to the eyes of the world – and to himself, and he is frightened by the knowledge and wishes quickly to be covered again. The soldier's despair is universal, but not to be talked about, a complicated strange disposition that it would take all history and all biology to explain. ...

there is a kind of hardness, a kind of animal violence developed by the experience of battle which surprised me, in myself – I was amazed to discover a part of myself which undergoes a wild primitive thrill at the sounds and sensations of a battle, like children at a fire, and is actually fascinated by the falling of bombs, and the slamming of shells and all the rest. (Letter to Geraldine Swingler, 4 December 1944)

... there is a well-known psychological trait that appears in anybody who survives a very prolonged experience of battle and war, I believe, very marked among fighter pilots in the earlier days of the war, that eventually he develops a sub-conscious feeling of shame for having survived. He feels somehow deep down that he oughtn't by all the rules to be alive, that he doesn't really belong to the living world at all, and that he should join his comrades who are dead as quickly as possible. (Letter to Geraldine Swingler, 2 December 1945)

Like Edith Sitwell's *The Shadow of Cain* (published the following year) the sequence conflates the story of Mary's brother Lazarus, restored to life after four days in the tomb, with the parable of the beggar Lazarus at the rich man Dives' gate. Swingler's Lazarus is a returning soldier who wants to die. Lonely, self-pitying and self-hating, he is suicidal with unhappiness. For the time being, Swingler had lost all faith, all hope and the only love he wanted. The 'stone eyes' are the faces of the insensible, alienated city, the unwelcoming face of Cold War London. But they are also the Medusa-eyes of Geraldine, who, like Penelope, does not recognise the returned Odysseus, sees only his rags. Because these are love poems to death, the 'mirror-white swan' (whose beauty he always associated with Geraldine) swims in these sonnets 'impassive' on the 'glassy image of death' The world had been emptied of meaning and purpose, bleached of colour, music and sensation, leaving only the weight of darkness and silence.

The second half of the book consists of a sequence of poems written while staying with Nancy Cunard in the Dordogne the previous July. After visiting the caves at Lascaux and Les Eyzies, Swingler immediately began writing 'Reflections on the Walls of a Palaeolithic Cave.' The poems answer the question asked in the Lazarus poems, 'How shall I ever expiate/The guilt of being alive?', demonstrating Swingler's return to living, re-born, *resurrected*. They are too a re-affirmation of the collective, magical, social function of art. The two sequences juxtapose their cave-imagery – tomb and womb – at personal, social, historical and mythical levels. The caves are at once Plato's Cave, the Freudian Unconscious, an Historical epoch, a nightmare of immolation, the Cold War winter, a dream of forgetting and a hole in the ground in Italy. The calendar vocabulary explores the psychological and social origins of war, between societies and within individuals. Afraid of peace after so much war, afraid of living after so much dying, Europe was terrifying itself with shadows in the cave-dark, instead of emerging into the light and promise of Spring. As if to prove his point, all the collections in the Key Poets series, including *The God in the Cave*, were ignored by the British press. The only exception was the *Daily Worker*, where they were denounced as 'the musty blowings of an unintelligible clique.'

Visits to Czechoslovakia in 1953 and Romania in 1954 did nothing to persuade Swingler that Communism was not in crisis. The revelations about Stalin at the 20th Congress of the CPSU in 1956 briefly gave him some hope, but it was clear that the British Communist Party was unable to acknowledge the scale of the crisis, and Swingler resigned from the Party. He was soon joined by other dissidents gathered round the *New Reasoner*, on whose editorial board he sat and for which he and Paul Hogarth edited a bicentennial Blake supplement. Edward Thompson hoped Swingler would be the poet of the New Left, but after twenty years of intense political activity, Swingler was suspicious of all politics. In 1958 he resigned from the *New Reasoner*.

The last decade of his life was spent in careless, fruitless, contentment in the village of Pebmarsh in Essex, visited at week-ends by friends like Louis and Hedli MacNeice, Edward and Dorothy Thompson, James Gibb and John Berger. While Geraldine went up to London to teach at the Guild Hall School of Music, Swingler stayed in the village, repairing motorbikes, working as a farm labourer and looking after their son, Dan, born in 1951. He was abridging books for children, teaching part-time at a local FE College, marking O Level papers, translating the *Aeneid* and writing a (never-published) book about the Lidice massacre. In 1961 he began reviewing for the *TLS*. By 1965, however, writer's block, financial worries, political despair, heavy drinking and medication for a serious heart-condition combined to cause a breakdown. The result was the release of a last, lyrical burst of automatic writing, including the valedictory epic *The Map* (broadcast on BBC Radio Four a few months after his death), and two late sequences of love poems, one for his daughter Deborah (whom he had recently met) and one for her mother, now married to John Mortimer. He died of a heart-attack in 1967, outside the French Pub in Soho. He was fifty-eight.

Randall Swingler was a writer of many contradictions. He was a high-caste Wykehamist in flight from his education and class, an ascetic and an aesthete, a Puritan and a Fitzrovian, a Marxist with a profound feeling for the

Christian tradition, a natural leader with a Corporal's stripes, a poet of the natural world who volunteered for the full ferocity of modern war, and a utopian whose work ended in hopeless despair. For all his contradictions, however, the poetry he wrote over a period of forty years was distinguished by an extraordinary consistency of vision and voice and feeling. 'All I want to do is make a huge single statement,' he once said, 'All I can do is make notes in passing.' Collected here for the first time, these 'notes' on his time and place and generation may be seen to constitute a single statement after all, sharing a number of distinctive, recurring, overlapping features.

First, Swingler was a lyric poet, writing lovingly about the English countryside long after the Modernist urbanisation of poetry. Robert Bridges, in particular, remained an enduring influence on Swingler, from *Poems* and the urban pastorals of *Reconstruction* and *Difficult Morning* to the dream landscapes of *The Map*. Moreover, the many magazines with which he was involved, from *Farrago* to the *New Reasoner*, represented an informal English line of opposition to Modernism, articulating other, more democratic, ways of responding to the challenges of Modernity:

> The artist is not a special sort of being, inhabiting a rarefied atmosphere beyond the exigencies of common life. Rather it lies in his essence to have more than usual in common with the generality of men. Consequently, while he strives to achieve the maximum of effectiveness in his work, that effectiveness, as with all men, will depend upon the extent to which he himself is a fully alive human being... . There are at this present time too many adept practitioners of language, expert in 'the organisation of experience.' But unhappily so few of them are alive to anything more than their own individual interests and closely circumscribed emotions that their work, fascinating as it may be to the leisured connoisseur of technical facility, will always be ineffective as a life-force in the development of man in society. ('Controversy', *Left Review*, October 1934)

Second, Randall Swingler was a late poet of Old Dissent, an English Puritan who hated privilege and power, property and money. He was the inheritor of a vision of England shared with Langland, Winstanley, Milton, Blake, Clare, Morris and Edward Thomas. The English Romantic idea of the poet speaking on behalf of a protestant people runs through all his public poetry, most notably in the songs he wrote with Alan Bush. For Randall Swingler, poets were Arnold's 'true apostles of equality', Shelley's 'trumpets that call to battle', bearing a special responsibility to testify against cant and hypocrisy, to bear witness to a vision of an open-shirted, classless Commonwealth which would liberate all human living, loving and creativity:

> The aim of Communism and the aim of Art are complementary. In every age, Art was the map of man's striving towards freedom and further social development, the whole of our culture is the mirror of the developing consciousness of man's needs, desires and aspirations. Art has always been on the side of freedom, the freedom that means the liberation of man's energies by organization, by unification of purpose. Communism's programme is not one alternative of many possible, but the only possible way forward in the development of man. It aims at liberating the energies of society and individual man from the waste and destruction in the conflict of classes by setting up the unified organization of the people of a classless society, in which value will be based solely on social function. Only by becoming actively implicated in constructing the future of society can the artist require the experience which will make his work important and effective, and himself a true liberator of human consciousness. ('Communism and the Arts,' unpublished talk, 1938)

It was not an easy task to hold to such an uncompromising view of the poetic life.

Swingler was perhaps the last major writer to be able to speak from within this native, egalitarian, poetic tradition. His poetry brought him no material rewards, and little critical attention. Having given away his inheritance to the Communist Party, he lived for most of his life on the edge of poverty, repudiating all the privileges of his class in order to live among the common people. He spent the Second World War in the ranks, refusing to apply for the commission that would have separated him from the ordinary soldier and the necessary horror of the fighting. Because of his refusal to change his opinions when they became unfashionable, the doors of publishers, editors and employers were closed to him after the war and he was victimised by both McCarthyism and Zhdanovism. By the time he came to reconsider the tradition in *The Map*, it was not surprising that Swingler believed it to be historically exhausted.

Third, Randall Swingler was a poet of prophecy and witness. He began as a Christian poet, and although he was for most of his adult life a committed and highly public member of the Communist Party, he never ceased to honour the Christian tradition, or to recognise its regenerative, historical potential, even during the worst years of the Cold War.

Fourth, Swingler was a poet of modern war. Few English poets wrote so well about the Second World War or so powerfully about the Cold War. Living in an age when, as he observed, 'politics is war carried on by other means', his poetry was implicated in the religious wars which shaped the century, from the Spanish Civil War to the threat of Nuclear annihilation:

> The last war started with people who wanted to fight and begot a generation that didn't, and this one began with those people who didn't want to fight and has begotten a generation that does, and there's your strange spiral of history, that has caught us somewhere midway in its curve, who loathe fighting but now we must until it's all finished and there's no more (Letter to Geraldine Swingler, 8 September 1944)

Fifth, Swingler was a love poet. His first book was a torrential sequence of love poems for Geraldine; among his last poems were love lyrics for Penelope Mortimer. More precisely, he was a poet of love thwarted by 'the monstrous issues of history', who knew that though love and private happiness must be subordinated to the demands of revolutionary struggle, no cause can ever be successfully advanced if it is not conducted by men and women who are emotionally whole.

Sixth, Randall Swingler was a poet of public performance. One reason his work is not better known today is that it was so often written for the specific occasion, for the concert hall, the stage, the radio, the little magazine, the open-air. An accomplished musician himself, Swingler provided texts for Benjamin Britten, Alan Bush, Bernard Stevens, Elizabeth Lutyens, John Ireland, Christian Darnton, John Sykes, and Alan Rawsthorne. His 'Music and the People' pageant was set to music by composers including Vaughan Williams, Edward Rubbra, Arnold Cooke, Victor Yates, Erik Chisholm, Frederic Austin, Norman Demuth and Elizabeth Maconchy; his musical pageant for the twenty-first birthday of the *Daily Worker* drew a crowd of 10,000 at Haringey Arena. The supposed antagonisms between private and public poetry are false, he argued, not least because the intimate poetry of the late Georgians still enjoyed enormous popularity, while the public poetry of the Auden group was read only by the initiated:

> The quarrel between those who say that poetry can only deal with the most refined of human feelings and the most rarefied consciousness, and those who say it must always appeal directly to the mass, is a false quarrel. While the small and large circle are opposed to each other, both are impoverished. ... We want poetry that we can read at home, that will enrich our friendship, articulate our sensibility to environment, clarify our knowledge and control of ourselves. We also want poetry

that can be cried in the streets, from platforms, in theatres; that will be sung in concert-halls and in pubs and in market places, in the country and the town. Poetry to bind many together in a deeper sense of community, to move them to action and to direct that action, to make it at one time vehement and wise. We do not want either the one or the other, we want both. ('History and the Poet', *New Writing*, Christmas 1939)

Poetry can and should also sing and shout, in the open air, in the theatre, in the concert hall. Poetry also whispers and murmurs, around the fire or in the ear of a single person. It depends entirely upon what community the poet feels himself to share, and to press around him, at the time of utterance. If he feels himself to be alone and isolated, he will talk to himself, and it will probably sound like gibberish. (Epilogue to *The Years of Anger*)

In the last decade of his life Randall Swingler certainly felt isolated. Lacking an audience for his verse, he was unable to write. But in the late 1930s and early 1940s, when the defence of England, democracy and culture seemed to many to be the same life and death issues, he was at the centre of an artistic and intellectual movement whose arguments were radical, commonsense *and* popular. Between 1936 and 1946 the argument that England would be changed by the need to resist tyranny, and could only successfully resist tyranny by changing, seemed to be vindicated by events. Though Swingler may have been a writer of contradictions, those contradictions did not belong to him, but to the age in which he lived. He refused to believe that he lived in 'tragic times', an easy excuse, he thought, for hand-wringing despair and inertia. It was his achievement to make the contradictions of his time – Peace and War, Love and Revolution, Art and Propaganda, the Country and the City – into poetry. And to the extent that he inhabited the central contradictions of his generation, Randall Swingler was arguably closer to its centre than those poets who, though better known today, could only watch from the sidelines.

I am grateful to Judy Williams for permission to publish her father's work and for access to his unpublished papers, and to Ruth Boswell for permission to reproduce the drawings by James Boswell from *The Years of Anger*. The poems appear here either in the versions in which they were first published or, if unpublished, are taken from Swingler's surviving papers.

Andy Croft

Further Reading

Works by Randall Swingler

Poems (Oxford: Shakespeare Head Press, 1932)
Reconstruction (Oxford: Shakespeare Head Press, 1933)
Difficult Morning (London: Methuen, 1933)
No Escape (London: Chatto and Windus, 1937) novel
The Left Song Book (edited with Alan Bush, London: Left Book Club, 1938)
To Town (London: Cresset Press, 1939) novel
The Years of Anger (London: Meridian Books, 1946)
The God in the Cave (London: Fore Publications, 1950)

Studies of Randall Swingler

Croft, A. (1997), 'Politics and Beauty: the Poetry of Randall Swingler', in *Re-writing the Thirties*, edited by Keith Williams and Steve Matthews, London: Longmans.
Croft, A. (1998), 'The Boys Around the Corner: the Story of Fore Pubs', in *A Weapon in the Struggle: the Cultural History of the Communist Party in Britain*, edited by Andy Croft, London: Pluto Press.
Croft, A. (1998), 'The Best of Corporals: the Italian Campaign in the Poetry of Randall Swingler', *London Magazine* October/November.
Croft, A. (1998), 'The Achievement of Randall Swingler', *Critical Survey* 10:3.
Rattenbury, A. (1978), 'Poems by Randall Swingler', in *The 1930s: A Challenge to Orthodoxy*, edited by John Lucas, Hassocks: Harvester Press.

Background reading

Beckett, F. (1995), *Enemy Within; the Rise and Fall of the British Communist Party*, London: John Murray.
Branson, N. (1985), *History of the Communist Party of Great Britain, 1927-41*, London: Lawrence and Wishart.
Branson, N. (1997), *History of the Communist Party of Great Britain, 1941-51*, London: Lawrence and Wishart.

Bush, A. (1980), *In My Eightieth Year*, London: Kahn and Averil.
Chambers, C. (1989), *The Story of Unity Theatre*, London: Lawrence and Wishart.
The Communist Answer to the Challenge of Our Time (1947), London: Thames Publications.
Croft, A. (1990), *Red Letter Days*, London: Lawrence and Wishart.
Croft, A. (1995), 'Authors take Sides: Writers and the Communist Party, 1920-56', in *Opening the Books: New Perspectives in the History of British Communism*, ed. Kevin Morgan, Nina Fishman and Geoff Andrews, London: Pluto Press.
Croft, A. (1995) 'Writers, the Communist Party and the Battle of Ideas, 1945-50', *Socialist History* 5 (Summer 1995).
Croft, A., ed. (1998), *A Weapon in the Struggle: the Cultural History of the Communist Party in Britain*, London: Pluto Press.
Ford, B., ed. (1994), *Benjamin Britten's Poets*, Manchester: Carcanet Press.
Hawkins, D. (1989), *When I Was*, London: Macmillan.
Hobday, C. (1989), *Edgell Rickword: A Poet at War*, Manchester: Carcanet Press.
Hogarth, P. (1997), *Drawing on Life*, London: David and Charles.
Lindsay, J. (1968), *Meetings With Poets*, London: Frederick Muller.
Margolies, D. (1998) *Writing the Revolution: Cultural Criticism from Left Review*, London: Pluto Press.
McCabe, J. (1999), *Alan Rawsthorne: Portrait of a Composer*, Oxford: Oxford University Press.
Poulton, A., ed. (1984), *Alan Rawsthorne*, Kidderminster: Bravura Publications.
Rattenbury, A. (1978), 'Total Attainder and the Helots', in *The 1930s: A Challenge to Orthodoxy*, edited by John Lucas, Hassocks: Harvester Press.
Stevens, B., ed. (1989), *Bernard Stevens and His Music*, London: Kahn and Averil.
Stevenson, R., ed. (1981), *Alan Bush: An Eightieth Birthday Symposium*, Kidderminster: Bravura Publications.
Thompson, E. P. (1994), *Persons and Polemics*, London: Merlin Press.
Thompson, W. (1992), *The Good Old Cause: British Communism, 1920-91*, London: Pluto Press.

The Years of Anger

I Premonitions 1936-38

SUMMER BEAUTY

At the arch of this dangerous summer
Coming already to the days when dust
Will rust the founting greenery,
The leaning country like a broken wave,
Choked and frothy with its tired glamour,

Coming to the beginning of fearing
The wearying of familiar surprises
New guises of the same hunger,
Languor of first quick lust,
Lost thrill of holding and hunting and despairing,

At this judged middle of my journey
I discern beyond its surface, reflected,
The disjected image of my power
Flowering in multitudes among lilies,
Still escaping its own sulphurous burning,

So I have come to the valley.
Galleons of cloud beat down the horizon
And wizened day shrinks
Among crinkled woods. The air
Stares and droops like a dispirited ally.

Love's last wondering sun who burst
Into my first frozen nature, lining
The skin of life and gushing
With rash juices runnel and spring and fountain
Of my mounting frame, has passed.

In its nadir the full fruit
Recruiting all lights, turning to golden yellow
In its mellow April, learned a serene pride,
Widening each way
Rays of prowess in a skyey pursuit.

Whose joy, swiftness and praise
And the dazzling feathers won. Now doubtful
The spout shimmers in air, halfway between
The green and communal growth
Of earth, and self's ingrowing lunar phase.

Slow to outgrow that vapid humour
A summer beauty idle over the pond,
I wonder what exhaustive fascination
That face, still and broken, paler,
Availed to draw the strands of light like homers

Back to itself. Always the ageing sun
Thunders behind my shoulder and waving
This grave audience of trees will advertise
The unwise invasion of time. Still I am checked
By a reflected image. No life begun.

RETURN TO REALITY

Therefore and for these reasons
I have left you, my summer spouse,
And further provoked the season
To lay its suffering hand
Upon your begging face
And to dissolve your house.

Sleep eternally in my house, you said,
The sky is slate and the earth tiled
With its enamel meadows: night
Will cup her silent hand above
Our closeness: thought will move
Around our walls like frescoes behind smoke
And we will watch the mischievous lights
Dodge in and out in the crouching villages
Where the great lorries come grunting by
Bearing top-heavy prosperity
Out of the northern smoke.

We will sleep eternally, you said,
Here on this hill. Armies may sweep the valley
Like winter floods: the world heave and subside
In its menstrual pulse. But we shall lie
Whole and eternal beyond the reach of the tide
Beyond the momentum of events, beyond desire
Beyond perplexity and need.
Sleep here, you said.

And for a season I had sleep
In your house. I gave you my body to keep.
You hung my thought like frescoes round your walls.
No draught disturbed your hall.
No foreign voices whispered on your stair.
When one looked in the mirror there was no image there
But yours. In all the corridors where I went
Your footfall doubled mine. And I was content
That all my hunting should come home to you and cease
And I thought, this is final and peace.

At the end of the year
I looked out over the valley. Rain
Filled it with tall advance.
When all at once to me appeared
Pressing his nose upon the window pane
A face of death. He said, You sleep well here.
If this is enough for you, this sojourning
Outside time's growth, then why do you remain
Above this wearying hill?
You could have deeper and endless sleeping
In my loving soil.

And I looked and the face was mine
Shadowed on the window-pane.
In that ghostly and hollow skin
Those darkly straining eyes
I saw what you had done.
And the old blood began
To tap faint messages upon his prison walls,
Remembering. And that is why
Bursting, my dear, the insidious glass
And through the illusion of your love's completion
I escaped your house.

BRUERN WOOD

Grey like a zeppelin the cloud arches over Bruern Wood,
The rooks circle beneath it in a black storm.
The wind is our messenger. He rushes before it
Delivering his frantic warnings everywhere.

But vainly, and vain is the rain's light percussion upon
The windows of the still-faced women,
The indoor women minding their own affairs
Like the haystacks under the heavy streams of cloud.

Subject to time between kettle and candle they move
And see flattened upon the daily paper
Actual European events as
Vague as the smoky summer mountains.

They peer with flat eyes of resignation
At war, whirling like this storm, silent and sudden
And heralded by frantic wind upon their sons
Unregarded as autumn
Whose dying trajectory wails through the sad air.

ELEGY

The rooks revolve in the hollow palm of heaven.
Cloudforms that are its lines of nervous life
Hardly react to the wind's Cassandra prophecies
The hills too relapse in a stony stoicism.

This is the height of winter. The bones are showing.
We know precisely upon what frame
Our solicitous life will burgeon, and no more.
And I return as music to its theme

To these waving trees that seem elaborately to weep
Against the ragged grief of the sky.
Always in sorrow, puny fugitive, I
Recur to meadows, trees and sky

Perhaps because their classic shapes of grief
Give all, ask nothing: but a human pity
Suffers too, and there's no conscious life
But has already its due of suffering.

So from this earth eternity of power
I derive, these are real hands
That pass the world's eternal mandate
Not the imagined father's, not in the bowels

The substituted warmth of the womb
But in the sources of the blood a living affirmation
Our consciousness, our spreading and gathering movement
Whose tree rooted in the heart
Is our true text of history.

For the blood is no wiser than the body
As the arm is not stronger than the head who guides it
Reason and emotion are the shape and tenderness of the same leaf
And a man's power is no greater than his belief.

IN THE SILENCE

In the silence while we wait for the guns to go off
Intrudes the poignant chattering of birds, the bluejay's laugh,
In the deserted orchard and the desultory humorous trees,
A momentary cameo of Nature's easy unhalting ignorance
That will negligently continue to push up the unhurried spring and grass
Through our own country's belittled ugly face
With its wasting haunted cruelty and the rolling hunger of gas.

And yet that negligence the apparently effortless chance
Which brings green and the wilderness of plenty
Is a false judgement in us who overlook the earth-deep struggle,
The hidden repressed juice, life fighting for entry into light:
Who overlook as well the background struggle of man, whose swords
Of assertion will no less push through the bald and bitter face
Of a war he never wished.

FEAR

Under the moon's whiteness the white-faced people
Await the swan-like visitation of fear:
They wait the faint whistle from the dimmest marshes
The fluttering membrane of the sky and the crinkling
Of the hairs under the belly. The clouds driven
Wayward and glistening magnify their movement
By the frozen stillness of the roofs. Like a hand
The wind reaches its gloved fingers through the nearest
Concerns of the self. The light like paper shrinks
And the timorous breath of those who simulate sleep.
The windlass of the hours is wound. Distant and harsh
Those wings begin their shrill suggestion. Love
By despair wakened remembers his hopeless demand
As the beak draws down, down the deepening heaven.

THE JUNE LARKS

That mute day the lovers on the beautiful mountain
Wandering wherever in salient grass, forgot
The answering curve of time. Forgot altogether
The hunger and the plenty that never meet.
Even all the fumes of war and the deathly peace
Like a rotten water surrounding the towns, had seemed
No truer than their pictures in the lake
Lovely against the round of the sky.
For the larks' sensitive tremor through their wild body
Made every nerve a gauze, that wavered
With the power flowing returning through a world
Of flowers and fiery air and flexible streams
Like fine hair dangling on the face of the rock.
And from the slain limbs of time, tomorrow stood up
As human. No declining dream who later
Would focus his flattening glass his queasy desire
Upon this peak grown legendary. But June here
Hiding her face in the blue air, at poise
Between larksong and planetary life, observing spin
Their small earth saturn-ringed, and round it
Curling his eventual generous hands
Death, like a great sea, lying.

ACRES OF POWER

Acres of power within me lie,
Charted fields of wheat and rye
And behind them, charted, too,
Brooding woods of beech and yew.
Beyond them stretch, uncharted yet,
Marsh and mountain, dark and wet,
Whence sometimes in my dream and ease
Strange birds appear among the trees.

The fields of corn are action's fruit,
Gripping the earth with puny root,
Their surface pattern neatly planned
Upon the chaos of my land.
Against the ruminating wood
They set a fence, but to no good;
The shadow and the sap of mind
Still weighs the harvest of my hand.

And the wild marshes and the hills
Shut out by the imposing will
Yet hurl their livid storms across
To smash the fence and flood the fosse
And all his dictates and his laws
Cannot restrain that surging force,
For the whole land is my power still,
Divided, fenced, but no less real.

And one man only mourning goes
By day through the stiff planted rows
By night through the tangled wood, to gaze
On the vast, savage wilderness.
The born surveyor, he that would
Turn the whole acreage to good,
Subject to one coherent plan
Dispensing the whole power of man.

But he between the fences dour,
This organiser of my power,
By rigid areas is confined
That sever impulse, hand and mind.
For he is only paid to see
That the fields grow obediently
And that the woods do not encroach
Nor the trees part to show the marsh.

For if the power that lavish there
Breaks into a sterile air,
Were planned and planted, fibre and juice,
And all my earth enlaced with use,
Then evil for his ruler's case
Whom to maintain in idleness
My fields of power are bought and sold
And all their goodness changed for gold.

Thus the land that is my life
Divided, ruled, and held in fief,
All the power it could produce
He cannot sell, but I could use.
And my surveyor, grim and harsh,
In secret now reclaims the marsh
That cultivated acres there
May bear a fruit for all to share.

AS CHRISTMAS WANES

As Christmas wanes, the interval of despair
Under a world that's waiting for the worst,
Concealed like an old well but always there,
Is opened to the air
And the widest joker knows it first
That history may be just but never fair.

The beautiful working of its perfect scheme
May come apparent to the pensioner
Like the interpretation of a dream
But to us all the same
It is the blood, the loss, the fear,
That will our thinking and our feeling frame.

The mind divided from the working body
Looks in the bowels and will find them foul:
The accurate response is never ready
And like a drunken lady
That foggy membrane called the soul
Totters along shamefaced and sham and shoddy.

It is not the gaiety nor the psychic hope
That saves us or renews us at this time.
Illusion can be blown to any shape
Of pleasure, wit or sleep,
Yet though it be intense as steam,
When it condenses, we shall only weep.

THE PRISONER

Round and round the prisoner goes
And his every corner knows.
Dreams he hides from, on the walls
Hang like bats. And hidden scrawls
Chart his rare illuminations
On the margin of his patience.

Day by day his quivering eye
Gazes on the passers-by
And his desperate hand appears
Signalling between the bars.
By night, in his own darkness caught,
He fills the sullen space with thought.

This he knows and this he sees,
Infinite complexities,
Useless all while he is locked
In zero from the world of act,
Useless all when he is dead,
With nothing done and nothing said.

I am that prisoner, who strives
To link himself with other lives
But always finds himself alone
Prisoned within walls of stone,
Whose mental world is thin and false
As shadows painted on the walls.

The walls of stone my parents built
By false respect and sense of guilt,
Upon the walls the painted gloss
Is compensation for my loss.
My love of life within the cage
Pent like a panther purrs with rage.

This prison and this iron gate
The safety of my class and state
Constrain the growth of hand and eye,
My dangerous humanity,
And what was love is made by fear
Hatred of all that comes most near.

Yet sometimes I have passed a note
In secret to the world without:
And tapping through the walls have found
Answers return from underground
Where lives the working multitude
Whom force and fraud have kept subdued.

And now no more my thought repines
In metaphysical designs.
My fingers bleed, my nails are raw
With tunnelling beneath the floor,
That we may meet and move at last
To storm this prison of the past,

And opened to the light of fact
Our thought may become truth in act.
For we could use these walls of stone
To build a city of our own
Where truth must work to make us free
And justice mean our unity.

THE POSSIBLE

Comrade heart, if ever you should be tempted,
Looking on the white and cheated faces
That pour from cinemas, the slackness of bodies
Endlessly acquiescent, walking the streets,

If ever you should be tempted, comrade heart,
By your own smallness, by your own longing
For quiet rivers, maternal hills,
And the solitary sun along the wrinkled sea,

If you should be drawn into the tragic dream
Of histrionic ruin, and begin to betray
The force of your ancestors unfolding
Their fearlessness like buds within your blood,

If you should be tempted to despair, remember,
Remember at once, and be humbled and quickened,
That already the lands live, where men
Spread forth their life like an ordered and opening flower

Where the factories and the growing machine
Compact as coral, no longer devour their flesh and time,
But like an enlargement of the general mind
Project the pattern of its will.

There all we fight for, is already growing.
They are sowing the fallow we have not yet broken.
Their pleasures are not hectic and yearning and unreal,
But vigorous as an accompanying wind, and universal and
overflowing.

So what your inner energy dreams, is possible too,
The power creating both dream and act. But you
Only by despair delay its trenchant action,
Only by saying "impossible" make it so.

PRAISE FOR THE ANONYMOUS

No one will ever know your names. You will never
Be inscribed on Rolls of Honour. You do not expect
A word of praise. Perhaps you will end your days
In desert prisons, the subject of casual sneers,
The indifference of the self-satisfied. Those who come after,

Who are riding the wave when it breaks at last and the foam
Dazzles with rainbow colours of the days of hope,
They will not remember who you were, far back
In the broil of ocean and out of sight of the shore
Who kept your course though the tide ran out against you.

Softly you held your honesty as phosphor its light.
You will create the leaders who will be known,
Who will shout like trumpets, roar into battle, their names
Scattering like sparks in the wind of history.
But it is you I praise, for deep in the cylinders
Your patient pressure will still be the driving force
Whom no one remembers, nobody ever knew.

AFTER MAY DAY

Out of the park the march has wound its way.
The bands are silent. The banners are packed away.
And homeward going, our hearts still sing the tune
For the people have held the streets for an afternoon.
Comrades, now is the time to remember: fine
As it is to come out with the thousands who follow our line,
To give the salute, to feel like a flood behind you
The press of the people whose needs both drive and bind you —
Fine as it is, it is easy to sing when the streets
Themselves are alive with singing, when the drum beats
The rhythm we want in us all; it is easy to show
Your conviction in shouting the slogans that all of us know.
What's not so easy is what comes after: the mandate
We carry alone into places where none understand it:
The patient explaining: the slow and tactful advance on
The forts of prejudice, the rigidly false assumption.
What's not so easy is to begin at beginning,
The embryo organization, the quiet winning
Of trust from cautious men, who have been sold
So often, their hearts and their hopes are equally cold.
What's not so easy is to be consistent
Both in the large affairs and the small commitments,
The unfailing punctuality, the ear to the ground
It's easy enough to speak the words that move
When the crowd is aroused and wants what you wish to prove.
That feels the rhythm grow when there's hardly a sound.
It's easy to lead in the open when the issue's clear:
These things are the rewards, that rarely appear.
What's not so easy is to lead in the dark,
From moment to moment knowing just where the spark
And just how strong, may be struck. For the real work
Is the work that no one sees, and earns no remark.
The life of the mole, patient, alert, precise,
Planting the true word in the secret place,
Never conspicuous except in mistakes:
This life, that will never be praised, is all that makes
May-Day and revolution possible. This at least
Is what is meant by being a Communist.

THE YEARS OF ANGER 17

II The Ordeal of Love 1936-40

LETTER I

The midnight streets as I walk back
Are half in white and half in black,
White in the light that night repeats,
Black-roofed and floored in day's defeat.

And black the shadows of my thought
Stand up against the white retort
Of all the brilliance I have known
Beside you in this stricken town.

This war will keep me waking long
To wrestle with the constant wrong
While heart and reason disagree,
Either impatient to be free,

Free of the curse that checks us here,
My fatalism and your fear,
Whose black denial intervenes
Like the angelic sword between.

Such are the knots of guilt and sin
Our history is tangled in
And cannot be untied again
Until our world is whole and sane.

This battle which they wage in me,
Desire and Necessity,
Can never be resolved before
Mankind has won the greater war.

Because the soil from which we're reared
Is poisoned with the rot of years
Our simple will cannot evade
The twisted root of fear and pride.

Therefore the love you make in me
Begets more vehemence to free
The world whose nets constrain us still
From loving with a single will.

LETTER II

And tender while you seem, yet hardness hides,
Something that still rejects and still derides,
Under your skin, that will in smiles agree
But still be incompatible with me.

The night recedes. The morning quickens. Between
Both lurks the hour of tension. Should he lean
And she be drawn? Or should he lead her on
Until she finds all in the venture done?

I only recognise behind your eyes
The tense foil fencing, the wary guard that spies
Danger of attack, that plays my thrust, but knows
It is humbled if it yields, resisting glows.

Time sets some limit to this. Suspension risks
A weightier climax than the issue asks.
Love knows his limits, but in check grows mad,
But while his act is simple, will not be sad.

Simple then let us be, while there is time,
For the mind does not wait but in its dream
Tangles desire into strange shapes, perhaps
To-morrow to torment us with this lapse.

LETTER III

Glittering and pleasant as this sun on the roofs
And yet unable to probe my deepest wound
Is your happiness and lightness
Our easy reflection of the day's brightness.

We have no share in the same war. You work
To emerge into loneliness from the shifting sea.
I on the other hand to merge
My solitude with the waves that gnaw its verge.

You yet believe that loneliness is freedom.
I know that having that, it is not what I want.
Freedom is what we have never had,
The active union of wish and need.

Freedom is then what loneliness cannot defend
Nor contemplation in the desert sand.
Only the acceptance of the need
Resolves our conflict, unifies by deed.

So freedom is final release from the personal limit
Active in history's unrejected power
Where personal death and personal praise
Become irrelevant as the sequence of days.

This I can say: though still the secret fear
Prohibits my clear resolve, divides my thought.
Am still distrained from what I would do
By the fear of seeming less, and hurting you.

You and I are on different sides of the wall.
You seek for what will make you whole,
I from the opposite pole
Fight against all that has divided Man:

Fight against all that now divides me from you,
All that has made of us two yearning larches
Whose branches strain but never touch:
All that has made the meaningless the true.

LETTER IV

Hands are producers, consciousness the consumer.
Between them is the rift. Power that should
Expand my knowledge of the good
In practice, and become
By consciousness of itself a greater power,

Finds itself now habitual behaviour
Subject to an imposed inhuman will;
And consciousness must still
Be only of its own confines:
Not unifier but enslaver.

So everything that separates you from me
Divides us two as well from Man
Renders our consciousness and power
More ineffective every hour,
Makes us more deathly as we are more 'free.'

Yet mind's consumption should integrate Power's production,
And we in thought-conditioned action
Know what we need by knowing what we are
And growing consciousness
Release a growing power.

So should we see
That not the difference between you and me
But mutual incapacity
Our common social isolation
Has brought about our sickly insignificant situation.

And you and I could yet attain
A satisfaction and simplicity
On the same side, in the same war,
Living as never lovers lived before
With the whole force of history in our veins.

LETTER V

You, my beloved, by the loved rocks sitting,
I know your fear and I know your fretting.
I know how this green tide sliding and receding
At the black cliff's foot, seems no more greedy
And no more vain in greed than your hard loving.

I know how I seem moody and unsure
Vast and indefinite as its uneasy power,
I know your thought and have no comfort to give.
You fear the whole devaluation of love
Which so darkly infuses the one act of living.

Yet remember too, it is your living I love,
Your thought and decision, your every act and move.
Your heart is nothing to me except its beating,
Your mind exists only in its noble fighting
For light and reason against mine, and all deceiving.

You are lovely now as you struggle, now as you weep
In the throes of knowing love has nothing to keep
Of any moment; only in making and awaking
Power for each hour of struggle, love in taking
The inevitable for truth, is free from grieving.

For you and I as lovers are no less
And no more than mankind. Love's distress
Has the same root as hunger's. Between you and me
That bondage is broken down, our unity
But makes more strong our part in all men's striving.

And you and I, my love, are no less welded
By acting in that world in which we are folded.
Are no less close by going apart
Since it is the longing for freedom from which our love must start
Whose silent passion is all our movement driving.

LETTER VI

If you are beside me when the sirens go
And I am called to fight for what I believe
And die, perhaps, that after me men may live
As men unchained, and into freedom grow,

I shall be brave enough, I know,
To take upon myself without regretting
The mud of war, the inevitable blood-letting:
And while your will goes with me, I shall not grieve.

More than aught else I fear your possible grief,
Casting its net upon me, halting my power;
Proving that neither you nor I
Have satisfied love's first necessity.

For love's satisfaction is not a thing of time,
Is not brought nearer by one additional hour.
Love is not love in anything more than name
While we have any loss to fear.

For while a part of either is possessed
That man or woman is whole by so much less,
By so much less is loved, for where is power
Imprisoned, there is man less mature.

Love liberates, by making whole.
Then if we have not failed, we have all we need
And we are whole now, and love is true:
There can be nothing to lose, of me or you.

So when that old reaction, driven to bay,
Spits its last poison against our rising life,
I shall be gladly obedient to my belief
And to your love, that freed such life in me.

LETTER VII

On the first day of snow, my train
Shuffles to London through the coated air.
Every sound is a thud on a deafened ear.
Sight too is muffled, for the long fields drift

Like wool into a woollen sky. The soft
Cope of cold oppresses every move
Like a cathedral silence. Trees in white gloves
Make decadent gestures. In a white calm I pass
Between two actions in my sealed compartment.
Suppose I were going to death, it would be like this.
I mean, suppose they struck: for the time being
Our world were frozen under mad repression,
The people defeated by their own despair,
And the champions of clarity everywhere
Herded away in trains to be shot and buried:
We should look out on the world as I do now,
Our valid work invisible under the snow:
Knowing it was over for us. We should have the same
Calm that I now enjoy. For action moves us
Like waves against the shore, forever outward,
Wilfully implicated in the natural movement.
But when stillness intervenes, it is to you
That I return, my solid ground of love
Where clarity has become articulate
In every detail: the sensible interest
In the immediate object finds a true
Unforced and unidealised delight.
Yes, we have formed the nucleus of our world
Which shall become the world, where freedom is
The understanding of our own desires,
The knowledge of our power; the active world
Is an enlargement of this. Love's one desire
Is to make whole, to stop at no division.
So what our love must liberate in us
Is power for action, the necessity
To make the world whole, that we may be whole.
Love needs no safety-catch. Security
Lies in our understanding. So, my dear,
In every intervening hour
To you I return as to my springs of power.
Love gets more children than grow in the womb,
More than the envious snow or the frost of fear
Can ever scotch; and such a generation
Of power to permeate the world
That death himself brings nothing to an end.

III Farewell 1937-40

ENVOI

Tree, thrush, lonely dark lake,
Still evening and magnificent classic swans,
Wait for us till the war is done.

Not now while the mind is diseased
And leans his wounded body upon your comfort,
Melts, wilfully forgetting, into what is not you,

But memory fraudulently evoked
By your recurring image: but remain
Silent and calm, uncorrupted by the mind's disease.

Till we return and if victorious
Real citizens at last, the body whole
Honest and vigorous, full with light,

Can see you and the world, as you,
Not images of our own desperate defeated life
But other than us, thankful for difference.

SUSSEX IN WINTER

This is my weakness and my pain alone;
To long still for the whole scene again
For the cold hills and the moveless deer
The intimate isolation, easy and secure,
The slow looks across the room and the music flowing,
Signal of an understanding which was not really there.

This longing for perfection is the snare,
Which locks out everything but its own desire
And makes a life of a single mood, forgetting
Even that love requires no permanent setting.
Death is the sole perfection, and even then
Only for the individual that's gone.

"Never" reverberates in the idle brain
For something gone which will not come again,
A fiction of the mind which never grew
And needed isolation to seem true.
That was not life, but dangerous and the last
Recrudescence of the seductive past.

Now that which grows wrestles with that which stays
Untouched by change, the hidden wall
Hovering about me, always ready to close
When I retreat defeated by history's ways.
For lapsing, our lives into early chaos fall
And the coffin is the last inhibition of all.

I write this in the station waiting room.
Slack eyes and bodies in the transitional gloom
Remind me of the agony of change
How man draws close, always aware of danger,
Pinned by his own ideas, and makes
A revolution with every step he takes.

SAD EVENING

In the still evening
When the remotest shadows glide
And the lion-like shadows
Leap from ambuscades,

Confusion and the dim mystery
Of fear is beautifully glazed
By the twilight of dying, the graceful
Posture of the blonde elegant day.

This is the saddest time for mortals.
Like a betrayal of love
The dusk is a mirror which can minimise
All human endeavour, even the warm blood's movement.

All vain seems violence and the riven muscular
Power of the land. Rivers glacially stilled:
The large clouds piled like petals: and vivid fires
Twitter and stumble in the thinning light.

The wind collapses. Noise melts. The rhythm
Of dying controls the air. And the sky is given
To silence and the charmed
Resistless flight of the unreal birds.

STRANGE FIELDS

Burning between the beanfields and the corn
And the long hills prowling on either hand,
Back to my country and my haunt of heart
I come like an exile on an illegal journey.

What can you do to me now but show my loss,
Hurt me with giving what I must reject?
I am condemned to the town. Its streets of war
Are my own veins of struggle, the ropes of blood
That net my hands —
               And O my loving land
How should we meet but with the twisted smile
Of lovers by hereditary disease
Divided once and now forever strange?

INTERIM

The corn will shade again and the blown grass
Be nuptial in my sight: the hidden hills
Suddenly look out along divided country
And all the equipment of a lover's summer
Will storm the ready sky to capture nothing.
This will come again I know, though now
The acquiescent forces lie in mud
Gambling among themselves, smoking away
The thin end of the days, almost forgetting
That anything is meant to happen. Life
Goes underground and does illegal work
For whose effect but history has an eye.

THE FIGHTER IS CALM

Nothing can indicate
With more cruel precision
The mind's divided state
Than this exorbitant passion
For self-effacing action.
Fear uses every defence
That honour may slip by
Responsibility
Suggesting every chance
Of danger and of loss
Or plunging desperate
Into the last abyss
To evade the perfect choice
The answerable voice.
Wherever mind or power
Seize the predominance
Where passion blinds the hour
Or thought withdraws into trance
Death has been sown in the grain.
Far behind action's line
The idle brood on harm
And the anxious heart
By hazard is torn apart.
Only the fighter is calm
Whose suffering flesh is joined
With the positive act of mind
And intellect and hand
Co-ordinately respond
Desiring the only safe,
Necessity of life.

MARCH, 1939

Man's joy is simple as the sun,
His misery tangled like decay.
For all that grows, is making one,
And all that dies, falling away.

And now this complicated doom
Only the simplest needs deny
Like sunlight in the morning room
Or spring or love or the March sky.

The weakling may be torn apart
By the fish-mouths of sickly hope
That somewhere from the ground will start
An unsuspected philanthrope —

These are the escapades of death,
The rumours of a change of heart,
A new world order built on faith
In all that has betrayed the past.

Still there remain the simple facts
Of war and hunger: and the power
Which greed in fewer hands contracts
Breeds pestilence and waste and fear.

Let spring and March speak in our ear.
Our need is simple: what we lacked
Was not the light to see it clear,
But courage and the will to act.

AUGUST BANK HOLIDAY, 1939

Come out on the esplanade where the butterfly blazers
Glitter as in a shop-window, all displayed,
The girls in trousers stalking like deer in a park —
What does it matter if the sky is hollow and dark?
Here is happiness! Here is the moment to forget —
BUT IF —
        to forget the weeks of worry and fret,
The unpaid bills, the inadequate wages, the ache
Of monotonous work for inadequate wages' sake —
BUT IF —
        forget all that! The small waves sigh.
Come down on the sand and find a place to lie —
To lie and pretend no holiday has an end,
To sleep in the sun, forget, dream, pretend.
BUT IF —
        No, don't buy a paper, they all say the same.
We don't want to bother with news. That's why we came.
We came to enjoy ourselves for once in a way.
This is our holiday. This is our day —
        Who is that man down there on the beach
        Waving his arms and making a speech?

        Don't listen to him. Come away, come away.
        Don't let him spoil our enjoyment today.

BUT IF —
        Oh what is he saying? I don't much care.
Let's go and try our luck at the fair.
The roundabout siren hoots like a cry of despair
And the swings go swooping out in the air
Away from the world, away from thinking at all,
Trying to touch the aeroplanes where they crawl
Like flies of steel on a wheel-blue ceiling,
See the sun give a flick to their wings as they're wheeling —
BUT IF —
        wheeling above the people who wave and cheer,
Wave like the bunting that flutters along the pier.

Machines are lovely as nature, the pride of man —
BUT IF —
   to-morrow machines will claim us again.
But to-morrow's a long way off. Let's take a trip
To the heathery hills, or launch a pleasure ship
To the islands of promise where cheating waters dream,
The islands that sink at sundown when all go home —
BUT IF —
   go home to work and the drudge of a day
And night that falls on want and uncertain pay
And a future that — Don't think of that! This is holiday.
 Why do you frown and run your hands through your hair?
 What is this greyness falling across the air?
 Thunder bends the horizon. It's going to rain.
 Don't be so moody. You give me a pain.
 What's that he's mumbling? What does he mean?
AUGUST BANK HOLIDAY 1914

The beach is chilly. I'm feeling cold.
Now children stop fidgeting. Do what you're told.
We'll go to the pictures. We've still got two hours.
The lights on the pier like burning flowers
Drop rustling petals into the sea
Golden dreams for you and me
Golden the dreams in the nights that follow
Something to remember in the long dark hollow
The hollow of life I hate and fear —
 Another holiday comes next year
BUT IF —
   Oh dark as the night sweeps in
With the tide and the moody crowds begin
To gaze at the sky where the searchlights intertwine
And the bombers are stealthy as germs now and the whine
Of sirens makes the lights on the esplanade
Look pimply and small —
BUT IF —
   We must catch our bus.
Let's get there in good time, to miss the fuss.
We've had a good day, we mustn't complain

BUT IF —
>   let's be thankful it didn't rain
BUT IF —
>   make the best of it while you can
BUT IF —
>   that's a motto for any man
BUT IF —
>   all good things come to an end
BUT IF —
>   just smile and things will mend
BUT IF —
>   to-morrow it starts again
BUT IF —
>   that's life, we mustn't complain
BUT IF —
>   keep it up boys, sing and cheer
>   Another holiday comes next year
BUT IF —
>   stop that thunder, I can't hear
BUT IF —
>   don't let me remember my fear
BUT IF —

>   BUT IF IT COMES?

But if the disaster comes, for which they're plotting,
Intending us to suffer for their gain,
Bidding us laugh to hide the crack of rotting
Planks collapsing under the strain,
Telling us all is well, the crisis over,
Turning our eyes away while they uncover
The hidden guns —

why then, we shall discover
That it is true, what we were told before,
That those who live by stealing from the poor
Will steal our body and soul if they can get 'em
Would turn our blood to gold if we would let 'em,
Starve, torture, prison us and call it kindness,
Make peace a desert and our freedom blindness —

Yes, if it comes, though we have much neglected,
It will not be the war which they expected.
For we shall accept what we have always known
That there's no power to save us but our own.
And we shall march, knowing the way we go,
And we shall fight, knowing who is our foe.

The points are changed. The train's on a different line.
Here we return to town, to take up again
A struggle that will decide for me and mine
Whether the future is mapped in peace or pain
AUGUST BANK HOLIDAY 1939

THE BEGINNING OF WAR

At the door of the world the thought of happiness
Looks back and leaves without another word:
A woman aged, who has made her last appeal
And failed.
          Now whirled in by a wind of horror
The dusk hangs over every house and the threat
Of plague with corpses and cordite in its breath.
Virtue is everywhere to be iron and man
Is admired for feeling nothing.
          Oh if within
This rock there is still running the lightest vein
Of water from the spring — oh if there is still a time
When the eyes can soften and the heart float
Like the sun on restful cloud — and oh if the skin
Still gives with an unsureness, not of fear
But of expectation — then there is yet again
The chance of youth, the lips adroitly parted
To utter hope like happy rain.

TESTAMENT OF AN ARMY OF FATALISTS

In London's quivering darkness
    A million of us lie
And feel the houses shudder
    And the trains grumble by.
Our morning's expectation
    Sinks like a sleeper's sigh
For while the year is waking
    We are about to die.

We who have watched it coming
    But hid it with a lie,
The hope that none believed in,
    The fear we daren't defy,
Now feel the nets about us
    Enclosing swift and sly.
We turned our face from living.
    We are about to die.

We heard but never listened.
    We sold to them that buy
Our senses with our labour:
    Then watched them fill the sky
With broods of death and darkness
    And never asked them why.
Now we have got our answer
    We are about to die.

They minted mind and vigour:
    They drained our bodies dry:
They trapped us in the marshes
    Of workless lethargy.
They blocked all roads to living
    And scotched the will to try.
Now as our final service
    We are about to die.

You who are coming after
    To whose unblunted eye
The sun showers down a future
    And the summer signals fly,
You shall not have to name us
    Either with sneer or sigh
For not in the war we wanted
    Are we about to die!

Massed in our veins the anger
    They could not mortify
Will to their final order
    Make this our last reply:
Though it is late for learning
    And death's what we learn it by,
Fighting our own cause only
    Are we prepared to die.

IV Battle 1943-45

THE EXILES

Those Spartans on the stony hill
Combed their long hair and oiled their splendid limbs,
Preparing to be beautiful in battle
Like a trained team before a football match.

Here, lounged along the sand, or shoaled
At the sea's fringe, whose acid blue
Burnished their bodies with metallic health,
Might old Herodotus think he saw them again.

Brilliance of body, yes, but look in these faces
Grown quiet with the strange awe of their time,
And meet the unreflecting core of their eyes,
Flint of necessity, stones of resignation.

Here all extravagance of mind
Is sweated out. They have passed through the furnace, felt
The slow squeeze of heat, the vulture blaze
That picks the eyeballs, whips the naked skin.

Apt to their poverty, the sand
Has rubbed away all sensual hunger, left
A bone-white pride of separation,
Like lizards, only cold of heart and blood.

Only in the rigid desert night
The moon seems to swell with so much released longing
And the deep sky draws up a faint miasma
From each man's individual dream.

In all this clamour of suspense, they fall
Silent as those who have already looked out
Beyond the polar extreme of man's endurance
Where Hate staggers on under the corpse of Hope.

Here they wait, any moment now
At a casual sign to snap the taut summer's skin and
Burst like the roaring forties, spat off the sea's tongue,
Into all crawling Europe through the gates of fire.

(Tripoli: July, 1943)

BRIEFING FOR INVASION

To-morrow, he said, is fixed for death's birthday party,
A gala show on the beaches, and all invited,
Fireworks and aerobatics and aquatic diversions;
To-morrow you can be sure of a grand reception.

At o-four hundred hours when the night grows sickly
And the sand slips under your boots like a child's nightmare,
Clumsy and humped and shrunken inside your clothes
You will shamble up the shore to give him your greeting.

Not all those present will shake him by the hand
But none will pass on without looking into his face;
The moment may seem chaotic, but be content —
A world has laboured for this supreme occasion.

Over your heads and over all crouching Europe
The sky will be lashed with sounds too huge for hearing
But to some listening inland it will seem like
The great inarticulate word *Freedom* howled by the dead.

Your skull will be filled with the hoarse breathing of death
And the gossip and chatter of all his ghostly devices,
The dust suddenly spouting with ferocious flowers
And the air canopied with a charnel smell.

And when the white sun retches across the land
The ships will litter the sea like deer at grazing.
But other and pitiful litter along the shore
The catspaw waves will lick and leave like vomit.

O love! is it worth it? And are the dead rewarded
With a bearer bond on history's doubtful balance?
And is the loss redeemed by a sunset glory
A sweet transfusion of blood to a new-born world?

No, it will never be worth it, nor the loss redeemed.
The dead die hideously and there is no honour.
The blood that runs out in the sand can only embitter
The violence of a fate that is still unmastered.

Even though some should slip through the net of flame
And life emerge loaded with secret knowledge,
Won't they be dumb, sealed off by the awful vision?
Or should they speak, would anyone ever believe?

Only this pride we have, both now and after,
Because we have grasped the fate ourselves created,
And to have been the centre of contradiction
And not to have failed, and still to have found it hateful.

(Salerno Bay: September, 1943)

HEAVY SHELLING AT NIGHT

1
Why did we laugh when we heard it coming?
Express train rush — hysterical shriek
And crash — like a fat woman pushed in the water —
And after with all the high air whinnying
Death's inexpressible lamentation
And again and again earth twitch and shiver
Like a horse's skin when the flies prick —
And the atoms of night split into glistening fragments —
Pocked in the earth like weevils, living and dead,
What should we find to laugh at?

2
Laugh, Boy, laugh!
Laugh at the noise of everything breaking loose
Laugh at the chaos of madness! Laugh
Because there's nothing else we can do
But creep in a pocket of earth and laugh
Laugh at ourselves, at our marvellous nerves and brain
With all its cells of wavering sensitivity
The ear tuned to delicate tendrils of music
The body shimmering to every nuance of love —
Oh laugh — laugh that all our centuries
Of mind, wrought, wrestled knowledge and art,
The subtle and wonderful thing that man is
Piling peak upon peak of civilization,
Have qualified us for this
To sit in a hole and laugh at the end of the world!

3
But the end of a world is always an anti-climax.

In the first light, when silence falls aghast
With deliberate miracle the reproving
Land slowly returns, unveils, unnaturally
Withdrawn and quiet.
                    And dawn unrolling
A ribbon of white silk seems ineffably pure,
Wonderful, intrinsic victory, the world

Hurled forward a whole historical leap —
And the last night's dead already lie transfigured.

NO SECOND FRONT THIS YEAR

Autumn drones on a sombre hornet note
Among the sweet-chestnuts and the little oaks,
An autumn without birds, the first autumn
We have seen for two years —
For the desert has no seasons, only quivers
Between the seven levels of hell's winter —
Perhaps that is why she returns with a cold touch
And only a bitter melancholy that clouds
Our veins like catarrh, with all that weariness
We have not felt till now.
                     But now we know
It is no use looking out across Europe for signs,
For winter breathes through autumn, and winter means
They will not come, not till another year.
And we feel suddenly forlorn and abandoned,
Lost in these hills, clawing and groping forward,
Another ridge, another month, another
Bitter, cheated, strained-to-exhaustion winter —
And because now our cold hearts must confess
There'll be no miracle to bring this thing
To a sudden end. We have seen the whole map of struggle,
The diversions, the broken bridges, the sealed exits,
We have even seen the weather chart
Of our own hopes and guesses and gales of rumour.
We know we deceive our own hearts because we must —
But there are no gaps, no half-way house, and no
Short cuts. The map shows only one road and that
The longest and the hardest, because we made it so —
And, Christ! the larger part of it yet to go!

(Mt Camino: October 1943)

THE LINE THAT DIVIDES THE WORLD

At evening the quiet hills uncurl
Sun-warmed, close, as old friends' faces —

Strange that there ever was a time
When we could walk on those hills, and I
By stretching out a hand
Could touch the face of my love.
We have forgotten now
The simplest of conditions
On which we accepted life.
The least of what was our due for being Men
Moulds now our most audacious dreams.
In this world man has no rights.
He creeps like a poacher on death's estate,
Quick with antennae sense of what's in the air,
And learns to read each trick in the uneasy grass.

Incorrigible outlaw, the heart
Stubbornly human, will not recognise
Death's government, quixotically true
To life's outmoded, half-forgotten laws.

It is not death nor pride
Nor any justifying beam of idea
That moves my mind now as I look down
Into the invisible chasm that parts the world:

What gives hope yet for man
And meaning to the mad horror or our time
Is the simple fact that when I look in death's eyes
I still see only the face of love, my love.

(River Garigliano: January, 1944)

INFANTRY COMING OUT OF THE LINE

So must the ancient dead
Have climbed from Acheron
Or Aeneas' ditch of blood,
Their ineffectual substance
Still spangled with fine dust
Like phosphor that reflects
And holds the wistful light
A little longer, a little
Longer — Brittle the tension now
Between the real and the dream
Dewed with the bloom of death
Still, these drained faces,
(Embrasures of the eyes
Frame the long bore of guns)
And every feature bleak,
The nerves withdrawn and hiding,
Blind walls of a beleaguered city
That has not realised
The siege is raised, the invaders
Gone with the sly night.
They do not look. They walk
Like blind men, boots shuffling.
Maybe one shouts a greeting
But the sound is detached, wild,
Has another meaning than ours
Like a gull's cry.
               Inside
The skull their riot begins,
The mob of memory straining
Against the cordon of pride.
Rest will be no rest
But a fear of falling, till
Sleep softly supervenes
And slips the knot of will,
Horror with laughter mingling,
And the frontier melt
Between despair and longing
And felt things be but things
Divested of emotion

And reason slowly wake
To find the world is still
The only world, and what
Was done and what encountered
Was the unavoidable run
Of life as it is given
To make of it what we can.
Dream-locked, grotesque survivors,
They will know least of all
How animal behaviour
Is made by circumstance
A superhuman feat,
And by historic chance
A month of hell becomes
In memory's colour-filter
Framed in heroic gilt:
Or what dim calculus
Works out the indifferent sum
That they should be the one
In every ten who now
Painfully to resume
The fallible of life
Limps back from Acheron.

(Anzio: March, 1944)

FOR WHAT CRIME?

Sadness of exile unavoidable too
Begins to feed upon his difficult will
For time, not distance, measures separation.

The wound he left has healed. New skin grows over
And her life shows a new face of which no feature
Is tinted by the recognition of him.

Between the lovers a glass screen has fallen
Whose spectrum sifts for each the other's life
Like an old map, gay with heraldic perils.

In their time's prison all comfort is reversed.
Despair is gentle when exhausted pride
Lays down the long-distance telephone at last

Knowing the wires are cut, all virtue gone
From the worst agony of trying to reach
His futile indistinguishable voice.

Perhaps, poor heart, you must learn for a time the art
Of valuing the dream above the real.
Dream lives in mind and always as you will.

No one knows what crime deserved this sentence
But none thinks of remission till the full time
Is served, yet after will require his vengeance.

Strange heart of contradiction by which we grow!
We look at life and find it intolerable,
Look into death and see the face of love,

Freedom takes refuge in indignity,
The lovers lose each other to be worthy of love,
And Man in the inferno finds the courage to live.

(Cairo: May, 1944)

THE GOTHIC LINE

1
Rimini Rimini even the ghosts of lovers
Have fled. All memory's dead as the air.
Only the slithering tanks more human than us
Can live in this grey pre-glacial waste.

Ah Rimini, no a phantom of rose remains,
Not an ebony gesture of an old ship in the sands.
Nothing. There is no sky. Volcanic fumes
And a dark smell oppress the mud.

Nothing lives here but crawls
Between black craters of gutted farms.
Earth like a sick animal
Sweats and shivers in a malarial fever.

And we, blind termites, lost to everything
But a mechanical instinct, creep on
Creep on, eating a way through ruin.

2
Now all my effort must be iron and anger.
For as you enter the region of struggle
The radiant arcs of force subtend a future
Which by their curve we measure,

But at the heart of tension all is blackness:
Every eminence of time is razed to the ground,
And at this moment of nothing where I pass
My chance of non-existence, I am blind.

Just for this moment he seems to triumph.
No bronze glory softens our haggard landscape.
Man fights and destroys without hope or love.
And if we live, nothing is solved:

Only the simple terminals will be sharpened
And the old antagonists come out of the wood
To face each other like the lion and the panther.
Nothing will be defeated but our fear.
If we live — But I who live by my love
And by my love create, feel, know,
Must enter this region where love cannot go,
Must in this moment be what most I hate.

And yet because it is my love which here I negate,
Because this instant's life is the knowledge of death,
Because we handle fate like a Bren gun and have learned to hate,
Life is assured, and some world will be saved.

(Coriano Ridge: September, 1944)

BETWEEN AGONY AND DESIRE

One evening when the moonlight flowed
Along the olive leaves like old music
And the crickets excited the air to hysteria
I lay on my back in the Italian garden

And the tree by my head became an old man
Whose body was refined by delicate shadows
Of agony, and his arms meagre as grasses
Drooped at his sides, giving his life away.

And as I looked in his face
So thumbed and pencilled as by centuries
Of ravenous weather, his thought became ravelled with mine
And as I breathed he spoke in the valves of my heart.

And said "I am watching."
       And then I knew his name:
He is called Dachau and his name is Million
He is called Buchenwald and Sachsenhausen
And before all is uncovered, he will have other names.

Name of the Nameless! Never can these stars
Be for me but the stigma of your wounds
Never these olive trees but the twisted image
Of your unseen and voiceless agony!
How shall we lift our heads above this tide
Of grief? Or how shall any world transcend it?
— But faintly, like my own reluctant knowledge
Denying indulgence, he spoke in the beat of my wrist:

"If you remember, remember only the anger.
Sink into suffering and there is only pity
In whose great eyes all virtue melts into tears
And even courage is a kind of pathos:

"Or reach after desire and you are caught up into dream
The bubble wish that denies satisfaction
Except the rainbow transfiguration of madness
Where the saintly idiots smile and gibber:

"But somewhere between suffering and desire
Starts the live current, and it may be anger,
The movement that is magnetism, heat and light,
The will that unifies, illumines, sets in motion.

"Not that poor hope which softens men's eyes
Nor the cheap death which denies it, claims remembrance:
But their last casual action that slipped between
Hope and death, their unreflecting greatness —

"Step by step necessity defines
Your will. You find when you hold your desire
It is not what you want, and victory brings you
A strange freedom which you do not understand.

"Do not remember the suffering, nor the terrible
Nullity of all our desire: only remember
The anger, whose waves of motion though unmeasured,
Ranged far enough to charge your soldier's memory."

And the moonlight rang like a gong: somewhere a spandau
Louder than crickets tore strips off the dark.
No joy, no bitterness, but an iron calm,
An unfenced road ascending without fork.

(Near Urbino: September, 1944)

THE DAY THE WAR ENDED ...

On the day the war ended
The sun laced through the avenues with lime-tree scent
The silver birches danced on the sidewalk
And the girls came out like tulips in their colours:

Only the soldiers were caught, like sleepwalkers
Wakened unaware, naked there in the street.
Fatuous in flowers, their tanks, tamed elephants,
Wallowed among the crowds in the square.

There is a moment when contradictions cross,
A split of a moment when history twirls on one toe
Like a ballerina, and all men are really equal
And happiness could be impartial for once —

Only the soldier, snatched by the sudden stop
In his world's turning, whirled like a meteor
Through a phoenix night of stars, is falling, falling

And as his trajectory bows and earth begins
To pull again, his hollow ears are moaning
With a wild tone of sorrow and the loss, the loss ...

(Gradisca: May, 1945)

NO PITY, NO POETRY

(to those who asked for War poems)

"The poetry is in the pity"
But there's no pity.
No fine words, no splendour of martyred truth
Can cover our gaunt Necessity.

What would you have us say?
I have seen communism storm a city
And envied another's future. I have seen boys
Suddenly eager in the moment of death
And men go into battle with the eyes
Of lovers. I have seen
The utter irrelevance of the body
When life has left it.

What do you want it to mean?

I have dwelt with the frogs in the kingdom of mud.
I know that man must always be too small
To grasp the enormous lever of his time
While his own power appals him. And I know
That most of us are learning a lesson too late.
But neither pride nor pity
Troubles our eyes within the limiting dream
Of finishing this war —
For if with no love
We aim but to redeem
The inherited debt,
    What could we more?

(Faenza: Christmas, 1944)

The God in the Cave

Lazarus or The Walking Dead

1

On the hither bank of battle
He made a deal with Death, to take away
The aching pack of Fear; should he gainsay
All hope, all expectation, all regret.
Death signed, and kept his pledge.
The Soldier laughed and sang in the sweat of hell,
And by sheer accident defaulted on his debt,
Emerged bewildered on life's further edge.
Haunted, returning to the source of hate,
He kicks the dust of ruin which he made
But finds no key; and is not justified.
He owes a debt to death and has not paid.
    How will he ever expiate
    The guilt of being alive?

2

Ah yes, he will be captain of his soul
All right, a dark prince taking no counsel,
But traversing all day the long routine
Of empty chambers in his heart's domain:
Walking, walking, with no one at his side
But the inept sound always following
Of someone hurrying to overtake,
Whose hand is always about to fall on his shoulder,
In this narrow passage between enormous dooms.
This is all so familiar that only now
When he is at last alone, the query grows
Curling maternal like a fern in his mind:
    Why is there no one with authority
    To show him that he has not sinned?

3

Because he does not hope to turn again
But has accepted that voluptuous sin
Which inspissates the world and seals him in
The ornamental garden of his pain:
Because the mirror is his magic lake
Which hides the subtle sword between the eyes
And parts the watcher from his loved disease
To hoard division for the mystery's sake:
The slow light filtered through the walls of skin
Like sunset on the desert, liquifies
Distance and Time; and conjures him to feign
Mesmeric sleep from which he need not wake.
    The hope of life will cease to aggravate
    Or death to taunt this beggar at his gate.

4

The dreamer on the sea-shore feels the drift
Of shingle and the silt of memory
As the sole marks of motion. Time is still
Because it has nothing to measure. The gulls are only
Brilliant poseurs in the chanting air
And the blind fish, charged with slick intuition,
Laugh in their languor with a lethal flicker
Where light is a twitch electric in leaden calms.
Deeply confused with all the vowels of fear,
His bird-track purpose lost in a rage of snow,
He hovers at the foam-edge; all his hope
Spell-bound in the dead past, he cannot choose
But take for god the immobility
Of time and the terrible silence in the mind.

5

Now I know why the sea calls in the night
And men are willing to drown in the clouding sound
Under the cliff! And why it seems to be God
Who calls out of the weeds of resignation
With the voice of a drowned bell! And why my sex
Thirsts like a plantain in a dry well,
Whose wilful blindness clothes a skin of eyes!
The streets pile up like a recession of mirrors
But never reflecting the ghosts who pass between.
For all that is real is the relationship
Between me and my city. But this is not mine.
Here I walk, an unpossessing ghost,
An unregarded lover who leaves no impression,
Not even his own reflection, in these stone eyes.

6

Neither the world of mind nor the world of men
Is a private park any more. Only the asylum
Has high walls. For the hermit in his den
Eternity is blank earth at burrow's end.
Let him admit that Fear defeated him
In that place which his talk can never leave
Where he awoke clutching his metal death
Compelled to gaze into its lizard eyes:
And saw the heartless chemistry of nature
Working his dissolution while he slept:
And saw Fear's infinite recession,
Always the larger image waiting behind.
And there, because his pride had failed to find
The ultimate fame of death, he hid his face.

7

There is nobody else in his world. He is alone now.
All other organic life which might remind him
Of anything outside himself, is dead.
The lovely woods and formal hills surround him,
And of course the enormous sea, without its monsters,
Comforts and peoples him with hypnotic murmurs
And the passionless pattern of a few lethargic birds,
All that is decorative of his fading humours.
He prefers to die slowly. That is all.
His grudge against time simply that it foreshortens
The spectacle of his own decay. He loves
Himself like one who meets years afterwards
The only mistress he never won; and hoards
That evening sadness more than all noon's ardours.

8

He hid his face, and so he hid his faith:
He sold his hope, and thus he lost his love.
Man without love leans like the sun eclipsed
On that dark segment. Though his right arm blazes
With an april vigour, what can be felt is the heart
Shrunk into duty like an ageing planet.
Man without love wastes the flat world he walks
And drains the red-eyed stars out of the sky,
An accursed huntsman with his sallow dogs
Scenting distraction under every hedge.
O flickering faith, this fortress of the lost
Is draughty harbourage when the harsh
And lambing wind calls for a test of action
And plucks the dead-leaf flames out of your hearth!

9

Glassy image of death, the mirror-white swan
Slides on the rugose water whose colour is fire.
The reedy swords of circumstance are still as time
And the long banks covertly leading the eye
Are only guides into an infinity of light.
Death of day melts the points of division,
Even the distinctions of love. The perplexed planets
Of human experience swim together and the grassy nerves
Wear each their sheath of comfortable shadow.
Oh is it only melting and disintegration
Can so disarm the caution of the heart
As to release the impassive swan-like image
To move without motive beyond and in the boundless
Orbit of a unresisting world?

10 ENDING

Time for closed hearts and secret sorrows
Time for covering the unhealed wound
Time for indifference to tomorrow's
Knell of feet on frozen ground
Time for the easy laugh and crisp assurance
The suavity of habit and known fashion
Time for mockery, time of endurance,
For turning the back on the public procession
Time for the exquisite agony of kindness
Time for the fakir to walk the fire
Time to envy the compensations of blindness,
For cellophane pillules of desire
Time for slick rhymes and glossy stories
Time for translation of effort into Chinese
To seal off the basement to save the upper storeys
To flood the forest and preserve the trees
Time to turn memory's key on the dirty cellar
And scorn the clichés of the lark ascending
Everything clean and dry as interstellar
Space. This is the happy ending.

11 BEGINNING

First the bright world, shifting its rags to show
Like Odysseus returned the hard limbs of the voyager:
Then the crisps buildings with their humorous angles,
The sun on them frosty, alert, and the sleek roads
With jovial buses rollicking early to work:

Then the faces of the people, every face
A map of life under the survey of Time,
The war-map with its harsh lines graved on resisting clay,
And on the malleable, quick and faint and ephemeral,
The prints of oyster-catchers on wet sand:

First the bright world surrounding, then the locked cities
With their moving cells, the current within them,
Circle against circle moving: and lastly myself
And the same circles moving within me, desire, and habit,
Coil against coil creating the tension of Will:

For what of daring joy, for what of careless
Glory in finding alive, first the bright world,
Second the people, and lastly myself are to blame,
Loving even unavoidable ruin, loving what must be
To make my earth, my world again,
        my love, my life.

Reflections on the Walls of a Palaeolithic Cave
(Lascaux-Les Eyzies, 1949)

1 INCANTATION

Out of the womb Man emerges
After the nine-month winter in the cave.
In a womb of the earth Man recovers
The seed of his living on the walls of the womb-cave.

The beast has a name which must not be said
For the speaking of the name is also a power:
The power to create in the cave of the mind,
The power to destroy and to devour.

That power none must take to himself.
For the evocation in the cave is a sacred act
And all must share the power which goes out from the hand
To draw the beast into the ring of knowledge.

To recreate is to know, to know is to subdue,
To subdue is to kill, and after killing to partake:
To devour, to be One, to partake of the life,
To beget new life in the cycle of the womb-cave.

2 THE CAVE-ARTIST'S PRAYER

Keep me mine enemy before mine eyes
That I may know my fear!
Map me his image on the ice-driven skies
Of winter waiting; in whatever guise
He may appear,
Aurochs or tufted bison or bellowing deer,
Keep me mine enemy beneath my hand!
Having him ever near
May tighter twist the double strand
Of mind and nature, somehow to expand
This ritual sphere
Where worship is but to kill, love only to devour.

3 MYTH

Splayed across these hills, they strapped him down,
His wrists looped by the rivers, and his feet
Fettered in fissures of rock. His head hung over
The valley and his hair darkened the cliffs
Like a forest of oaks. Five hundred centuries
They pierced his writhing body with spears of ice
And lanced his flesh with the white bolts of the wind
Until the earth gleamed with his blood. At last
They left him for the moon to salve, his skin
All glossed with dewy sweat, shimmering like gauze,
And spangled with a cicatrice of stars.
This they did to avenge their haunting shame,
Made desperate by a glory they could not name,
And cruel beyond relief by the wild pain
Of a beauty they could neither understand nor attain.

4 LANDSCAPE

Sleeping on their sides by the water
Where the sleek rivers, Lot, Vézère, Dordogne,
Sweep impassive around their haunches,
The bristly hills like a herd of rhinoceros
Wrinkle in sleep.
    But will they sleep for ever?
And will the silken rivers throw
So nonchalantly their languid loops around
Alluvial land grown green with kindness?
                              Man,
Take courage! Nothing you can do
Could make a winter of this world
Like the primeval struggle between these two,
Should the rhinoceros hills awake
And the mastodon rivers rear their hood of ice
Cracking volcanic sinews. What you have twice
Surmounted, master you must again!

5 THE INNER DARKNESS

Every night is a winter for the body.
Hidden from hazard in the pristine darkness,
In the deepest mysterium of the skull
The priestly dream is traced on the rock-walls
To hoard the wish which waits for active summer
And so initiate the young in the blood.

Nightly too Earth creeps into its cave
When the moonlight makes rock-walls of the sky
Where the magic stars strike out compelling symbols
Only half-understood. So where the body
Must descend, is all Man's winter ever,
Nightly to discharge its darkness and be ready for light.

6 PURITAN CHILDHOOD

The house of childhood was a world of rooms
Each one a separate virtue. The small back garden
Sunny with naughtiness our stifled Eden
Over which always the winged lion of Goodness
Posed heavy paws above us, and his thunderous
Mane made lurid all the coloured landscape
Of pleasure, and the sun's forehead malarial.
How delicately we trod the fire-breathing grass!
How cautiously contained our web-like flesh
In terror of being trapped into happiness!
While the long cold hands of the black father, Sin,
Palpably pressed upon our cringing shoulders
Rooting our knees into the blessed stone,
Rigid, remote, and utterly benign.

7 CHURCH

Dumb as the beasts repelled by dangerous light
They enter the stone forest of their night,
And stooped beneath grey heaven's bomb-proof awning
Approach the hanging god whose mercy lies
Also in stone. Around his fluted thighs
The long leaves of their prayers, like picking fingers,
Scratch and corrode. For here the hunted god
Is hanged for ever on the cave-wall, whose trodden
Floor bears marks of feet defeated. Morning
Stretches above them like a slaughter of beasts
And the blood of day on the membrane window lingers;
Where they, the devoured, to worship the final kill
Of man eternally hunted, and for the feast
Of death, return to the womb-cave their tomb.

8 RESURRECTION

Now that the summer centuries of Man
Are augured and the weighted air is drilled
With doric columns of frosty and summoning light;
And in our misty vaults the rattle of feathers
Tells of the pigeons departing; those bowed heads
Vowed still to darkness and fear, divide the dream
From daylight action. The mouth of the cave of sleep
Is zareeba-ed with swords, and the sun is the enemy.
O better the great bull who showed us strength!
Whose terror was tinder to man's pride; in whose recognition
We were reborn into summer light! For winter and sleep
Is the node of waiting and preparation, at length
Set like a trigger-spring at dayspring to leap
To the summer test in the sun's keen decision.

Uncollected Poems

SONG OF THE HUNGER MARCHERS

We march from a stricken country,
    From broken hill and vale,
Where factory yards are empty,
    And the rusty gear for sale.
Our country will not thrive again,
    Our strength is not for use,
The bubble of prosperity
    Has never come to us.

    Then rouse to our tread
    When you hear us marching by;
    For servility is dead
    And the Means Test too shall die!
    Though they think our spirit's broken,
    Because we're underfed,
    We will stamp the Starvation Government
    Beneath the workers' tread!

We pass through sleeping villages
    And poor and struggling farms,
We pass through towns where factories
    Are forging war and arms.
In towns and fields and villages
    We see it more and more,
How the boss exploits the worker
    And drives him into war.

And this Employers' Government
    Is hoping for the best,
To set one against another
    By the grading of the Test.
They would train us in their Labour Camps
    For action against you,
But we march for the working-class,
    For we are workers too.

Remember, fellow workers,
    Who earn a wage to-day,
That they'll throw you on the scrapheap,
    When they find it doesn't pay.
All you who are employed,
    Making cartridges and bombs,
We'll be marching side by side,
    When the final crisis comes.

BEFORE MORNING

Lean down, sun,
Dash with your golden wrist
These mists away.
Let us know
The harsh horizon
And
The contours of our woe.

Strike from the eye
Sick hope, the cataract
Of complaint.
Help us descry
The fact
And knowing, fight not faint.

MAN LIKE SUN

Stretching forth to clouds, mountains, and a land
Sleep-locked, lifting the heavy leaves of death,
Man like sun arises, dark through days
His power condensing. Simpler than grass his breath
Hung first at lips, diaphanous. The ways
Of the wind distrained his hair. Personal desire
Shaped him. Youth and the summer marriage
Fulfilled the image, that lusts and fears, like fish
Here and there fretting his inconstant nature,
Might fall away. Now beyond the soft barrage

Of time, knows he must turn, his lakes of wishing
Steeped, and feel the protective past, with hands
Of a ghost, recoil from the hard trust of his loins.
For he will pass through the sea, whose creature
Movements beat now like the widening quiver
Of light through his attestant blood. Will join
Many together in the welding of a new love.

ESPECIALLY WHEN I TAKE PEN IN HAND

Especially when I take pen in hand
And watch the white chaos of paper
And rivers, contours, grow more complex and
Finer than a spider's navel-spinning,
Especially as the world grows under
My fingers, its limit always known,
This page's edge, but growing; then I brood
Upon mountains throwing off into easy valleys
The condensations from the sky
Of my imagination, upon the white ridges
Like a serpent's wrinkled back, upon the snow
Reserved but still proud, dazzling all climbers
With remote beauty: and upon the lakes
Where birds rest and call and make
Their inspired and rhythmic flights. I look down
Upon a powerful veined land, upon
Flesh where the power is drawn up, gathered
Under the skin, knotted in knolls
And curling muscles of the hills. I see evening
And morning visit. I see the abrupt silence
Of the moon. I see movement and waiting.
I am the creator. My power is here.
I look upon no landscape but my own being.

From ENTRANCE TO THE CITY

Looking about me I saw a curling country
Of hills and valleys like a heap of snakes,
At the edge, beyond their heads, the magnificent mountains
Like clouds; and at first a comfort like falling water
And universal delicate sorrow
Sank out of all my veins.
I was joined to this hill with roots like a nipple
To the breast and I thought the plains
Were flowing with waves of light like eternal lakes
Where cranes flew up out of the enormous grasses
Freighted with legends, and the curious grebe
Darted and elegantly towed their icy reflections
And sunlight floated warm and rich on the grasses
Buoying their seeds. And I thought for a time
I was alone and joined with this delectable
Land. But I was wrong.

For looking longer that landscape came
Within a new focus. Not snowy were those mountains
But rolling trains of smoke; under the hills
Furnaces glared like lions and the hiss
Of their running metal was a serpent's laughter.
Thicker and blacker were those hills forested
With slums than with cat-like pinewoods, and the rush
Of people passing in the streets, the crush of their feet
Denser than any wind over summer grass.
Not cranes in the air slanted, but planes
Side-slipped from the hanging clouds
And ran out, easeful, on to the polished grass
Like ducks on water, leaving their whale-like hangars
White-bellied behind them. And I knew
That I was not alone. That the same ring surrounded
Me still with their eyes.

From SPAIN

In Spain the valleys are golden in the sunlight
And gold suns glow in the orange groves.
The olive fields with their soft yielding colour
Slope quietly down to the silver beaches,
The bracelet of the glittering sea.

In Spain the mountains are pencilled finely
Against the vividly happy sky.
The idle herds, the donkeys on the winding tracks
Wander out of time. And age stands still
With beauty in the placid mountain villages.

In Spain the starved peasant stands like a stone,
Immobile for a moment on his harsh soil.
A third of its yield each struggling year
Goes to an owner that never sees it.

In the long moonlit Spanish night
The people stroll along the avenues, happy and careless,
The women flash their eyes leaning from windows
And the young men sing to the poignant guitar.

On Sundays in the arena,
The shouting surges through the hot crowd like wind in corn.
The toreador pirouettes before the lunging bull.
And the smiling grandees incline their noble heads.

In the Spanish towns, on the boulevards,
The workers stroll idly in the evenings;
The workers throng the stuttering factories;
Starved, swept into houses cramped as a pigeon-roost,
Darker than caves, nests of disease.

You who live in your exclusive island,
Do you really not understand
What is happening here?

Do you still dream dazedly of a land of castles,
A golden mist on the horizon of history;
And a savage, passionate people
Among whom murder is quicker than a lizard's tongue,
Bloodletting easy and thoughtless?

Oh, come nearer, lose your superior caste a moment,
See here Democracy, all the hope of a people's growth,
Straining and breaking its chains.

THEY LIVE

In your hesitant moments, remember Cornford and Fox
Looking across the valleys and the romantic rocks
Not even moonlight could make remote or magic,
Nothing nostalgic, nothing tragic
By the proximity of death:
No, but for them the trenched ridges
The machine-gun nested ledges
Were a concrete form compelled
By the same simple will,
History's pattern of struggle: by whose breath
They fought, and died, as it happened,
But wholly to live, our impulse and tradition.

Surely they knew as they wrote
That freedom is but wholeness;
For one alone a thing impossible,
For who shall be whole except mankind is whole?
A thing therefore for which they fought
And fighting found, and left as a light for us
To shame our pettiness, our indecisions,
To fuse by its certainty our divisions
And make us greater than we are
By showing what we might be
And by their young and unregretful star
To stab us with courage and confidence
Daily and nightly.

FRIENDS WE WOULD SPEAK A LITTLE OF THIS PERFORMANCE

I
Friends, we would speak a little of this performance.
You have heard the intricate orchestra,
The warm horns were curled like snails, the cunning flutes,
The sweep and shiver of the violins,
Intense and varied as the play of your own nerves;
You have heard the piano
Vaunting its brilliance before the chorus.
We here, in trained co-operation, spinning the pattern;
You there, in your hushed rows, listening;
Over us all the activity of music,
Like a web of invisible colours.
      And this web
Is something men have evolved in their living together,
Their mechanic skill adapting the instruments,
The enriched imagination controlling the skill
Into a harmony of sound.
And, thus exchanging a wordless currency of thought,
Men are changed, are somehow enriched,
Discover within them latent power,
Know their own fears and desires better than before,
And knowing, can better control.
They that have experienced this know well
That music is something that man needs.
      So has man's history
Out of his need developed the power,
And out of the power knowledge;
For power and knowledge must ever grow hand in hand.

II
Yet in our day the influence of thought
Is caged and bonded, like a bird
Whose wings beat in a vacuum.
Music itself must fret like a pent flood
That cannot reach the thirsting fields.
The utterance of the human spirit
Is something which can be bought and sold

As a mental luxury, while the poor hunger,
And their minds are warped and stunned
By years of slavery and servile education.

And those few, in whose hands
The reins of power are gripped,
Hold the lives of millions harnessed,
Jealously hoarding their wealth and privilege;
And fear the liberating impulse and the uniting spell,
The revealing beams of knowledge that all art begets.

These are they who propagate subtle falsehoods
Daily, like poisonous gas, to corrupt opinion.
These are they who, whenever they see truth,
Unfolding in summer flower, and men in hope
Banded together to loosen the collar of oppression
And to beget happiness at the expense of cash profit,
Stamp it out with the violence of their law,
Strengthen their frenzied grip, cry "Faster! Faster!"
To the mills that grind man's labour into profit;
And to the hounds that guard their parks of privilege
Cry "Fiercer! Fiercer!".

Their throne grows narrow, the gulf gapes for them.
Their fury increases as despair seizes upon them.
For they shall fall, fall, fall for ever,
Their rule and their practice shall be stamped from the earth,
The soil shall cover it, its chains lie rotting in the furrows.

Only in death shall it be fruitful, only its utter
Annihilation shall cleanse the world, shall leave the giant Man
Enormous in freedom, shaking his lightened shoulders, rejoicing once more
That all his powers are turned to the goodness of all,
And the unfenced fields and the towns like hearts beating
With regular pulse spread about him in generous peace;
And love is the law and Man in the pride of his will
Giving his all for all.

III
What shall we do, then, other than sit and weep,
Other than sink and let the music seep
Through mind and marrow like a summer sleep?

What shall we do, for whom no drug can still
War's felt crescendo, and the human ill
And our own sense of helplessness most of all?

Art is no drug, nor yet oblivion's river.
Music is the mind-changer, the life-giver,
The future's design, the release of new endeavour.

Come then, there can be no more sides than two:
War and waste for the privilege of the few,
Or a share for all in all men make or do.

Therefore, friends, who sit here waiting and fearing,
Know that in this fight only is the assuring
Of your fulfilment, abundant and enduring.

Upon our heads is laid such destiny
As none knowing can coldly cast away.
Man's future is to be fought for in our day.

TRIUMPHAL SONG FOR THE PEACEMAKER

Bring out the cracked drums! Dust the dented bugles!
Spread the worn carpet for his angular feet.
Lift high the torn flag and the rusty eagles!
Here comes the conqueror to the judgement seat.
Merchant of honour, barterer of peace:
See the certificate of his smooth transaction,
And cheer his salesman's tongue, his broker's face.
Surely he's buying shares in the next election!
What did he pay? Only a people's freedom,
Only some chunks of land that were not his,
Hoping the mortgage on your safety may
Never fall due till smug and safe he lies,
Oblivious of gout and bolshevism
Decaying like his system in the clay.
Hail to the technique of the false alarm,
That bold device by which you get us scared
By threat of war for which we're unprepared,
Then fly to save us from the imagined harm
And while we gasp in thankfulness, can spread
The nets of tyranny about our head.
O worthy triumph of that great tradition
Of monstrous lying that keeps in position
A government that does nothing but sit still
And gather up the profits in its till!
Bring out the trumpets! Blow them till they crack!
Bang the big drums until they break in two!
Put the soiled carpet down! Our conqueror's back
Waving the paper which has mortgaged you.
Give him due honour. He'll not be surpassed.
This latest fraud, his biggest and his last,
Earns him a proper epitaph: 'He sold
The world to save his power and his gold.'

AFTER THE POGROM AND THE STENCH OF BLOOD

After the pogrom and the stench of blood
Reeking with lustful fervour and the mud
Of the rich man's praise and the pert monkey's lewd
Encomiums of Nazi fortitude,
Is there some shrine, sanctified by the state,
Where the great Nordic heroes congregate
And putting all humility aside
Boast of their victories with proper pride
(Ten thousand children bombed in open fight!
A million women homeless in a night!)
But keep their longing ardour well concealed
For glorious death upon the battlefield.
And somewhere near, black-coated, I am sure,
The obsequious toady creeps across the floor
To lick their boots and vainly beg for scraps,
Barking a playful protest, and perhaps
Whining of peace, or any other name,
Thankful that he has sunk too low for shame.
And when their dreams confront them in their sleep
Whose shadowy perils from their slumbers keep
These thunderers of totalitarian war,
They call this Chamberlain and shout for more.
At once by careful blandishments betrayed
A neat democracy is before them laid
Already with provocation sauce made hot
And spiced with a mock communistic plot,
Devoured beneath the toady's tears of brine —

Hail! new Valahalla! Oh heroic sty!
Ask yourself heroes, when will democracy
Rise from the dish, turn and devour the swine?

ADVANCE DEMOCRACY

Across the darkened city
The frosty searchlights creep
Alert for the first marauder
To steal upon our sleep.

We see the sudden headlines
Float on the muttering tide,
We hear them warn and threaten,
And wonder what they hide.

There are whispers across the tables,
Talks in a shutter'd room,
The price on which they bargain
Will be a people's doom.

There's a roar of war in the factories,
And idle hands on the street,
And Europe held in nightmare
By the thud of marching feet.

Now sinks the sun of surety,
The shadows growing tall
Of the big bosses plotting
Their biggest coup of all.

Is there no strength to save us?
No power we can trust,
Before our lives and liberties
Are powder'd into dust?

Time to arise Democracy
Time to rise up and cry
That what our fathers fought for
We'll not allow to die.

Time to resolve divisions,
Time to renew our pride.
Time! Time! Time! Time!
Time to decide.

Time to burst our house of glass,
Rise as a single being
In one resolve arrayed:
Life shall be for the people
That's by the people made.

BALLAD OF HEROES

You who stand at doors, wiping hands on aprons,
You who lean at the corner, saying: "We have done our best,"
You who shrug your shoulders and you who smile
To conceal your life's despair and its evil taste,
To you we speak, you numberless Englishmen,
To remind you of the greatness still among you
Created by these men who go from your towns
To fight for peace, for liberty, and for you.
They were men who hated death and loved life,
Who were afraid, and fought against their fear!
Men who wished to create and not to destroy,
But knew the time must come to destroy the destroyer.
For they have restored your power and pride,
Your life is yours, for which they died.

Still tho' the scene of possible Summer recedes,
And the guns can be heard across the hills
Like waves at night: though crawling suburbs fill
Their valleys with the stench of idleness like rotting weeds,
And desire unacted breeds its pestilence.
Yet still below the soot the roots are sure
And beyond the guns there is another murmur,
Like pigeons flying unnotic'd over continents
With secret messages of peace: and at the centre
Of the wheeling conflict the heart is calmer,
The promise nearer than ever it came before.

ON SOME WHO WERE KILLED FIGHTING IN THE INTERNATIONAL BRIGADE

Damn all we ever wrote
    In searchings of the heart,
Unravelling the pampered knot
    Of youth's arrested growth
With emphasis on Art.

All that is changed indeed.
    For Death has intervened,
And while we slept and fed
    And nursed our ways of mind,
They fought for us and are dead.

How could we ever guess
    These ordinary men
Behind their calm and ease
    Hid a heroic sun
The power to change our days.

There was one had a gay mien
    And a gay tongue
The words danced to the tune
    When his heart sung
That will not sing again.

And one was serious:
    We chaffed his earnest face
To watch the slow smile grow,
    A child's incredulous gaze
To whom all seeing is new.

And one had subtle hands
    To make of metal or wood
Instruments of all kinds
    Turning the useless to good
And hard men into friends.

And one had an easy way
    That passed from hand to heart
As honest currency
    Wherever men were met.
Him they will miss today.

We who fought out with them
    Our common lot as men
Had still so little dreamed
    The bud which hardened them
Would come so soon to bloom.

Their dying implements
    Their goodness in the round
Which life could not present
    While from the same ground
Our roots took nourishment

The seed within the flower
    Is shaping next year's bud.
The action of this hour
    Creates to-morrow's mood
And to-morrow's power.

Now they are the earth for us.
    Their image rests more real
Than the swift change of days
    Was able to reveal.
Their influence is their praise.

For the ultimate division
    Of living truth from lie
Is the crass inhibition
    Which makes us fear to die,
Corrupting every decision.

But absolute opposition
    Of life affirmed against loss
Achieves such liberation
    That value becomes the force
Which storms the new position.

The seed within the flower
   Has burst already to bloom.
So life is given to ensure
   Our life, for the living come
To knowledge of their power.

MAKE YOUR MEANING CLEAR

Rise now you long exploited,
And let your voice be heard
In answer with Dimitrov,
And this shall be your word:
We will not fight for profits,
We will not die for pay,
Nor let our rulers drag us down
In ruin and decay.

Rise, rise, rise, working people,
And make your meaning clear!
Our foes are the exploiters.
Our battleground is here.
And peace shall end what wars defend,
The rule of greed and fear.
And peace shall end what wars defend,
The rule of greed and fear.

They bid us fight for freedom;
But all they ever gave
To Britain's working people
Is freedom to starve or slave.
Democracy's their catch-word
To send our sons to die.
We hear them use it once before
And know it for a lie.

Truth is a thing we'll fight for,
To save the world we make,
That we ourselves may own it
And rule it for our sake.

We rise and give our answer
To the makers of all wars:
The people fight for the people's right,
Their just and only cause.

SIXTY CUBIC FEET

He was the fourth his mother bore
    The room was ten by twelve
His share was sixty cubic feet
    In which to build himself.

He sat and learned his letters
    With forty in a room
And sixty cubic feet of draught
    The Council lent to him.

At fourteen he must earn a wage
    He went to pit from school
In sixty feet of dust and gas
    He lay and hacked the coal.

At twenty-two they told him
    His freedom was at stake
He left his sixty cubic feet
    A soldier for to make.

He slept with seven others,
    The tent was pitched on clay,
The rain ran down the hillside
    And drenched them night and day.

He lay and coughed his heart out
    In sixty feet of damp
At last when he could hardly stand
    They marched him out of camp.

They brought him from hospital
    They bore him home alone
In sixty cubic feet of deal
    That he could call his own.

They buried him with honour,
    The bugler blew Retreat,
And now he claims of English earth
    Some sixty cubic feet.

DRINKING SONG

The pub is the place where good comrades are found,
For the day's work is done so we'll call one more round.
Be it cider or guinness or fine tawny port
Or gin by the gill or good ale by the quart.

    So lift up your elbows and lift 'em up high
    And tip up your glasses till the heel taps the sky
    We'll drink to each other and drink to the day
    When working men and women have it all their own way.

Here's a plague on the brewer who waters it down,
Till you can't tell the difference 'tween bitter and brown,
And another on the Government that taxes our beer
While profits are mounting by millions a year.

Damnation to the martyr, the saint and the prig,
Whose bladders are too small and whose pride is too big.
And the worst we can wish them is the hell that they fear
A tropical country where you can't buy a beer.

Here's a health to the Red Army whom Hitler detests
And the kick in the panzers we'll give in the west,
Here's a health to the Soviets where the lads own the land
And here's to the day when all workers join hands.

Here's a health to our freedom and may it grow great:
When we take a hand in controlling the state
We'll clear out the fakers and the fat profiteers
And throw all the big-wigs outside on their ears.

Then all may be happy and work with a will,
For we'll own the factory, the farm and the mill,
And when ale's brewed for drinking and not for profit's sake
We'll put plenty of hops in and avoid belly-ache.

Z RESERVE

All the greyness of the autumn air
Sobers the afternoon. Respectable trees
Stand in subservient outline at their places
And the quiet shorn fields, their load discharged,
Temper my restless eye. This dangerous season
Of reconciliation might succeed
In balancing weariness against despair
And fixing on the torn and hungry face
A sort of death-mask of content. Already
I know that I shall never touch to blossom
The spring's exasperating buds of desire.
Already I am learning to crystalise
Pictures and images in the frigid mind
And value more the limpid glass of dream
Than all the musky gropings of the body
And obfuscating sense. I, like the year,
Have missed my harvest in the deadly rain;
My shoots were cankered by the unseasonal blight
Of war, and struggle into bewildering light
All rank and twisted. Action gross and raw,
Clumsy and too late, cancels the innocent bud.
Bitter the fruit that's forced out of its season.
Now only in the darkness of a cold
And contrite earth, my spirit sinks in stillness
Mourning and musing over the lost green dream,
And I who should look out in the russet comfort,
The humoured fullness of an achieved harvest
Now gaunt with failure, haunt like the homeless heron
The standing floods and rotting vegetation
Of a spoiled summer that will not return.

RETURN TO A BATTLEFIELD

No one, who was not there, would know :
Now that along the valley the sunflowers blaze in rows
And the ravelled red between the glinting maize
Is only tomato-fields. But to my eye
Those sunflowers are perennial monuments
Along the arc of fire where the shells fell
And tossed up transitory flowers of death
The day we lay in the ditch and talked of war's end
And the surprised young world that would waken to our return.
Up the hillside the stone-coloured olive-trees
With their smoky leaves, twist in arthritic age
Petrified into gestures of man's pain :
But clothe this soil with the same vaporous pelt
As the mortar-bombs that morning, falling
With a flat hungry bark in the forest of death.

Oh ! Earth has done them proud, whose bones
Lie under Camino's crown of stones
Putting out all her memorials to perpetuate
Even in flash of flower and smoke of leaves
Only the glory, the fierceness of their ending.
No one would know now what it is that makes
The tomato-fields barbaric in reckless red
Or weights the vines with their rich melancholy
And dry leaves folded like a hospital matron's hands.

But I can hear clearly now
Out of that soil the whispering bones respond
The voices still familiar :
               "What have you done
With the dream that brought us here? What have you done
With the world we promised to change? Do you remember
The pledge that justified your survival?"
And then I know
That I could become more dead than they. With them
It is only the bone that is dead. The earth is their flesh
And every year grows green in the sloughing of grief.
All they have lost is fear and the crooked bone.

But in me only the bone is alive, must watch
The slow decay of the will, the inch by inch
Retreat of the nerves, the death by shame.
"Joe, are you still our comrade? Are you true to our pledge,
By which, our one survivor, you became the heir to our lives?
What have you done with the world for which we died?"

What have I done but capitalise
An alien grief, angling for dividends
Of pity? Naked Lazarus, flayed
By the whips of fear, have tried to invest
Their legacy in foreign undertakings,
Waiting for other's work to ease my woe.

No, I know it. I am not of you yet.
I have not crossed the river, nor taken up
The changed life you have left me. Not till the dream
That lit your eyes with a fiercer flame than battle's,
That seared the shame out of man's mortal hate,
Has grown into this world, and all our cities
Blossom with your memorials like the vine and olive
And plenty and happiness is their natural air —

Not till then can I return to tell you
The pledge is fulfilled and I can join your rest,
And sit in this ditch and remember
With glory and laughter
The day I saw Communism storm an Italian hill.

THE WINTER JOURNEY

I The City

The city rustles like a rookery at evening,
The haunted city whirled in the smoke of worry.
The winter fog divides us. In private rooms
Important men contract their business.
All of us are minding our own affairs.
The taverns are full and the streets
Are like canals of hurrying water.
All of us are minding our own affairs.

If you bring money or business to this great city,
Or pacts or promises, or an evening's diversion,
If you bring fear and the whip, or wink and gesture,
Welcome! welcome! Enter the race!
If you bring food or finery,
A chance of easy money, or a lordly appearance —
Come in my friend, come in and sit by the fire.

But to us who bring for you nothing but a burden of trouble
Entering empty-handed, exhausted with travel,
Carrying only the weight of a new life,
The child in the womb — the wind is sharp and unfriendly.

There is only room for those who can pay in advance.
But for us with the builder's hand and the challenge of love —
No room in the city, no room in the world,
No room, no room, no room.

II The Journey

It was a wild journey they brought us,
A harsh lesson they taught us,
The yawning heat of the desert, the crags of terror,
The nights of exhaustion, the days without water,
The crawling hours that seemed to make no progress —
We hardly knew our direction, nor why we travelled.
One morning came the summons that bade us depart,
And we turned our backs upon home, setting out in the evening.

At first the road was level and we thought it easy,
But the second day the storm broke, away to our right,
And we barely escaped the torrent in the bed of the river.
Then all night long the hail beat on our heads
And the storm shrieked down on us like a wand of lightning,
And we had almost thought we would be defeated.
But we looked in each other's eyes and drew closer,
Remembering the burden we carried.

        We were very weary,
But the greatest ordeal was to come. On the sixth day
We came to the great ravine, where the very sky
Exploded upon us, and the rocks howled their hate.
And we could not have endured it, but for the new life
Already quick and stirring in the womb, and the thing
We believed in more than our own safety.

At last we saw the city, and for the gleam of a moment
The sun leaned down and touched it so that it seemed
All builded of light, and we thought the promise fulfilled.
But a screen came over the sky, and the evening grew cold,
And as we climb the street, the doors are closing.
Ev'ry man shakes his head and turns away
To shut himself up again in his old concerns.

But the child will be born, though none will give him shelter.
The city is thick with suspicion and evil rumours,
The look of fear, and the hand under the counter.
The child will be born in the streets, in the straw of a barn,
Even if the stone eyes of the city are sealed.
And we — must we make all that journey again?

III The Sleeper in the City

A wind stirs in the city like a reminder
Of something we must do but have forgotten.
The starlight on the sleeper's face
Disturbs his dreams, and when he wakes,
Knowing that something has happened, something is born
Tonight, but where and what, he cannot tell.

IV Mary's Song

Oh white-robed city sealed in winter night,
Sealed up in glassy light and stony faces,
Are you afraid of the life that we have brought you?
Is it your fear which shuts the door?

What does it mean that you send your princes to lay
Their power and wealth and privilege at his feet,
If you will not open your doors of love
And take up the future in your parent arms?

What is the price of life in your market now?
And when my child shall stretch out arms to me,
Which shadow shall I see along the floor,
The cross of death, or blossoming tree?

V Chorale

Winter it may be in the streets of time,
And all in vain, and all in vain,
They made that journey through the waste and wild,
Unless we make some place to lay the child
That will be born, that will be born
This Christmas in the season of the heart.

MY MISTRESS PLAYED

My mistress played
And every finger to one jewelled note
Was pearled.
You might have thought each phrase
A tendril of her hair translated
Into a curl of air.
And yet her face so still and rapt
As if the rivulet of sound
Washed its fine gloss into a watered stone.

O when she is caught
In that complete and limpid atmosphere,
I know
She is no longer mine,
Nor ought to be, but with all human
Kind is intimate.
I know, yet still in vain protest,
Since her frond and dapple grace
To me is most of all desirable then!

TO GERALDINE

In the day you may be
Single and lithe as a whip or hazel wand,
In the day you may be
Whole and round as a held note,
You may rustle your leaves of laughter in the sun
Be salty and sharp as crystal or sea-water,
Cold and glancing as the light off blades of grass
In the day you may go wild your own way.

But in the dusk you must grow soft as amber
Glistening like a stream in poplar shadow,
Let the darkness of your body grow luminous
As earth that sips the light at the end of day
Dewy you should be to the star-fingers of desire
And passive with a moonlight lustre; like the panther
You should move shy in the leopard-light of candles
Delicate as fallow deer among branches,
In the night you should grow soft
As a sword in the velvet sheath of darkness.

This way you share the pulse of light and dark;
Of stone and water counter the proud nature;
Shine and glow with the double faculty
Of gift and giver, of flame and flame's tinder.
This way you win both the world's love and mine,
All summer's delectable swallow, and my arcane swan.
Move with the rhythm of light, be all you have
To be, beauty and beauty's maker, human and woman.

MILLIE'S SONG

Hatred of all the world! Hatred of living!
Hatred of Man, and all his making and giving!
Hatred and Fear are the props of your sterile state,
The lust to destroy what you dare not help to create!

What are you doing here with your pale pretences
But setting snares for the lonely, the feeble senses?
Leave us our alleys clean. Get out of our town,
Before we tear your tawdry scaffold down!

Listen. Let me say it as plain as I can.
To be alive is the dearest blessing for man.
He loves the world who works with hand and wit
To extend his mastery over himself and it.

Ah! You have no monopoly of dreams;
For through all our daily striving the vision beams
Of a world where we're all of one heart, and unafraid,
A dream to be forged in truth, a world to be made.

Why should I wish to escape to your vile asylum
When the morning sun says New, and the night Welcome?
Not in your mirrors I look for what day denies me,
But in my own hands' promise and the dawn horizon.

That is my answer to you and your web of shadows
That will only catch Time's eunuchs and Fortune's widows
But you'll find that the sun of the living is sudden and bright
If you dare to open your Fair in this town tonight!

CHORUS

Life's a tapestry of rhyme and reason,
Line and colour, work and play.
   The earth is given for
   All men to enjoy
But gives no more than we create.
   Nothing comes to those who wait.
   Be the master of your fate.
Go, meet the promise of the day.

Mind imprisoned is a wasting sickness.
Man united is a king.
   Throw down the barriers!
   Let the daylight in!
Set Fancy free from sin and hate.
   For it's we who must create,
   Good or bad, the web of Fate,
Who make the dream a living thing.

Life's a quality of dream and daring
Conjured out of earth and air
   And he who loves the world
   Loves his fellowmen
In their fulfilment find his own
   But who flees to the Alone
   Desecrates his blood and bone
And wastes his spirit in despair.

LONDON NOCTURNE

With the blue of autumn in the boughs like a ghostly bloom
And a dying memory clouding the waters of the mind
On a Sunday evening I look over London's loom
Of coloured vapours like patterns of oil on a pond

Musing on the strange comfort of melancholy
When loss is known at last to be irrecoverable
And grief is the settled temper of the body.
The madness of the happy in parable!

THREE TREES

(For John Gawsworth)

Behind my house stands guardians three,
An oak, an ash and a willow-tree:

An oak for strength, an ash for thought,
A willow to watch my feeling heart.

Forty years long my oak has grown
Rugged and reaching and rude as stone,

As many years my ash has bent
To the smooth winds of argument;

But in between, in autumn yellow,
Weeping leans my broken willow.

IN THE LABYRINTH

Why were we ever taken in
By Theseus' tale? It's all too thin —
That sly stroke in the dark, the quick
Getaway by a girlish trick!
There was no evidence but his.
Besides, his subsequent faithlessness
And that unconscious perfidy
Of his black sails, gave him away.

There's no undoing, no forgetting
The monsters of our own begetting.
We know now we can never slay
The Minotaur. In open day
He must be met, and by the Will
Outfaced, outstared, and brought to heel.

THE BALLAD OF HEROD TEMPLER

Plague and Pestilence, Famine and Flame
The coward's weapons, the madman's game!
Shall this be done in England's name?
    The Princes of death have found their man
    Herod Templer rides again!

Plague and Pestilence, Famine and Flame
On those without defence or blame:
Who will redeem our England's shame?
    Sneering at Freedom's millions slain
    Herod Templer rides again!

From dying West to dawning East
Templer boasts the mark of the beast
Spreading the germs of a life diseased:
    Blazoned with the brand of Cain
    Herod Templer rides again!

The baffled beast balked of his prey
Savages everything in his way:
Villages burn and crops decay
    For planter's profit and tin-king's gain
    Herod Templer rides again!

Where is our people's ancient pride?
Under what heart of stone can hide
The faith for which our fathers died?
    Shall Freedom's victories prove in vain?
    Herod Templer rides again!

Lions of England, rise in your prime!
Show to the world till the end of time
We will expunge the Nazi crime!
    Wipe from the sky this hideous stain
    that Peace and Freedom shine again!

Lions of England, rise in your prime!
Malaya's ravagers in your name
Stand condemned of the Nazi crime!
    Wipe from the sky this hideous stain
    That Peace and freedom shine again.

YOUR TRAIN HAS GONE

Your train has gone. Carrying you to a land
Where the lines are clear, and the strong issues of life
Look obvious in the penetrating sun.
Your train has gone. The long grey platform lies
Like a deserted sea-beach, with the waves
Of your departure lapping uselessly
Against the impervious edge.
              And I left standing
Here in the centre of this difficult country
Clogged with too heavy an awareness
That more than the atmosphere is fog, remember
What we have always said, and try to believe
That neither time nor space can ever unweave
The strands of that loving work, or working love.

THE HARVEST OF PEACE: A CANTATA

1   Korea

*A voice was heard in Ramah
   Weeping and great mourning
Rachel mourning for her children
   Because they are not.*

The voice of one crying in the wilderness
Which the bombers have made, making straight
The way of the Lord: the voice of the mother
Crying in the wilderness which was her life —

   "Make straight the way of your Lord
   With flame and sickle of steel make straight the way
   Over the bodies of ruined children make it straight
   The path of Gehenna through the future land!"

And the bombers heard and laughed at the joke
Laughed like hyenas in the desert night
Their laughter riddled the hills and blasted the trees
And left the splintered chimneys standing
In a rubble of bones. The bombers laughed and sang —

   "We bring them civilization
   Blood turned to gold, the incense of corruption,
   The spice of disease. We bring them liberation
   From the thongs and throes of life. We bring them Peace
   In the plumed silence towering into the sky
   Where even the air is dead as an ash."

2 The Soldier's Mother

This year we shall not pull the flax
The ragged oats are turning black
This year we'll build no barley stack
    My son, my boy,
Till ever you come back.

This year the clover fields are let
The tools left out to wind and wet
The apple-branches groan and fret
    My son, my boy,
We'll have no harvest yet.

This year the grass grows rank and high
Lorries and guns go slouching by
And bombers haunt the haggard sky
    My son, my boy,
And you could tell us why!

Surely if all our love enjoyed
And all man's work and wit employed
Is to destroy and be destroyed
    My son, my boy,
Then all our life is void.
    All life is void!

3   Elegy for the Stricken Harvest

 Droop Summer droop
Your ears of promise and your buds of hope
Scatter the stricken seed on poisoned air
Droop down you overladen apple-trees
Droop down you bomb-shaped pears
 Droop down droop down
Aster and iris droop, and oh!
Let cedar and beech droop deeply down
 Where once we played.

 Droop droop! Your heavy heads
Will not be garnered in.
      This year
 There'll be no harvest here
 No seed sunk in the earth
 Only the seed of wrath
 The fermenty of fear.
      This year
 The weevil of despair
 Has drained the acorn. Blight
 Bleaches berry and nut
 Canker parches the air.
      This year
Young eyes will burst and gush with more than tears
Down fleshless cheeks: the frame of man be bared
Like a skinned bird and in its cage of swords
The cindered heart appear.
      This year
A bloodless sky will stare
On cities like a mouthful of rotten teeth
In a tongueless land.

 For this is the year of the bombers
 The year of the locust of fire
 The year of Herod
 The year of the child-murderer
    This is the year of the Lord
    The Lord of lies!

4 The Trained Killers

When I have scoured this earth, which is not mine,
And scored its barren flesh from end to end
With tank-driven furrows, do they expect that Truth
Can be sown like seed, or a way of life
Planted in rows like hop-bines trained
On dead stakes of the past?

Who will be there to see it? And what will be left
Of any way of life when this work is done?
For look how we live now, who crawl in mud
Like blindworms, coated with a carious skin
Of animal fear and all the equipment of death!

What is their Truth but a tuneless lament
Over an inner torment? Their ultimate knowledge
Is but of meaninglessness, the last despair
Coming full-circle with never a sight of the centre.
And how should I defend a disbelief
Against a living faith?

I have survived to learn that civilization
Means the control of superior ways of killing,
More complicated forms of death. The thing
They call my honour I see marketed
By little boss-eyed men with the minds of eels
Sinuously noosing human feeling in coils
Of supple double-sided deprecant words.

One thing I know. I have not begun to learn
What life or liberty are. And that long learning
Seems too difficult now. So it is left me
Here to sit and savour solitude
Like a man polishing a gun in the thin silence
Before he blows his brains out.

5 The Advancing Light

Day's funeral pyre
Burns bitter red
And late or soon
The harvest moon
Reflects a fire
Not wholly dead

The light that dies
In broken storms
On the far side
Of time's divide
Is seen to rise
With open arms

Let those who fear
Recede with night.
From time's morass
The wakening mass
Draws every near
The advancing light.

6 *The Song of the Wind*

There's a bright wind blowing in from the east
Like a scimitar shearing the fleece of the mist
A wind like a rocket, a wind like a spout,
        A wind a wind
                A wind to find you out!

The wind's in the city, the wind's on the land.
He scatters the leaves with a jocular hand
And tosses the skirts of the world with a shout:
        "Be sure be sure
                Your sins will find you out!"

In the streets of the wealthy he's running amok
And laughing his way through the tenement block
From castle and cloister he's routing them out
        Be sure be sure
                The wind will find you out.

He's blowing the newspapers over the town
He tweaks at the posters and tears them all down
All pomp and pretence he's delighted to flout
        Be sure be sure
                Your sins will find you out.

And you who seek power by the peddling of lies
Will waken one day with the sun in your eyes.
We're beginning to know what your game is about
        Be sure be sure
                Your sins have found you out.

And you who affect a superior stare
A cynical gesture of saintly despair
The wind whose existence you hold in some doubt —
        Be sure be sure
                The wind will find you out.

You madmen whose creed is bomb, batter and burn,
Take care that the wind does not suddenly turn
And blow your own venom back into your throat
        Be sure be sure
                The wind will find you out.

But you who can feel from the catch in your breath
The defeat in the air for the squadrons of death
Go warn all the neighbours to join in the rout
        Be sure be sure
                The wind has found you out.

The wind's on the mountain, the wind's on the plain.
He rattles the curtains and bangs on the pane,
A wind like the laughter of life in the mouth
        A wind a wind
                A wind to find you out!

7 *The Turning World*

The world is a globe, and the world turns
One face to day, one face to dark.
Somewhere the sun rises. Heart
Believes again in worth of work.
Though the poles freeze, the equator burns,
The world turns, and every part
Must sometime know the signal mark
Of unimagineable dawns.

Must I go east to find the sun?
Is there no more meridian?
Is the arc broken that should span
The morning and the evening man?
The human world, the human name
Though many-sided as a gem
Is lit with the same inner flame,
Is woven without seam or hem.

Our hope to certain morning grows
Wherever man looks up and sees
His realm expanding like the day's
Unfettered trade-route through the skies
And in the sun's impartial blaze
Out of the single-hearted maze
Of human thoughts and human ways
Each several hand contends to increase
The total harvest of his peace.

8 The Awakening Forest

Darkness closes over the city of Fear.
No leaves like hands folded in benediction
Smooth the forehead. The patients lie
Smarting in their own sweat. Thoughts
Pace up and down the empty streets.
Loneliness like a brittle frost
Holds up the atmosphere between finger and thumb.
The leafless forest stands without stir
In perpetual winter. Every building
Separate stands. No roots of love
Link in the earth, or draw the sap
From the labyrinth of the soil.
Peace is the singing soil
Beneath a dovewinged sky. The dark and plangent
Earth sown with million on million
Springing seeds, million on million
People signing with their living blood
The final Paid to the bill of yesterday
Million on million over the globe
Of the world turning from shadow to light
Signing Yes to life and Welcome
To to-morrow. Buds thronging
The branches of the human family-tree
Buds to burst into leaf to roof
The sky with dovewings, olive-shade,
The green peace, the re-awakened
Forest of man's love.

A ROSE FOR LIDICE

Lidice lay unknown
In the lap of a lying world
Lidice worked alone in the core of stone
Lidice had grown from the blood of the earth;
Coal and steel were bone of Lidice's birth.

Fate chose it for hate's gangrened fury.
Hate said: Wipe out the name!
History shall abjure it!
Ah, the brave dust blew round the world;
The air flooded with blood of roses.
Hate had ploughed up the soil. Love sowed it.
Where the murderer's heel stamped on the eyes of children
The gardener's fingers fashioned them into roses.
Love is a ring once broken proves all untrue.
But the shed petals are a token of the bud's renewal.

While man's love grows and blossoms in time's ground
Lidice hangs, a garland round the cross of the world.

From THE FALL OF BABYLON

Winter. Earth's contraction.
The weary womb expelling
Its problematic birth.
Night. When love is naked
And the blind life springs.
Honesty in the dark.
The greatest daring
Men can yet commit.

    Ask the shaggy ass
    Or the slow cow
    Why in barest winter
    We look for a new birth
    We listen for that message
    Which light would not allow
    And the widening year disproves.

Suppose we have conquered day,
Harnessed the years of light —
Still the protestant heart
Drums in its own night.
Earth speaks through the ass of the brain,
The cow of the milky senses :
The shepherds of imagination
Gather their puny lambs
Of childish understanding.

Babylon's wise men
Offer their several answers
As ransom for their pride,
But only see their own gifts.
In the night around them
And the naked winter
The ass who knows he's an ass
And the slow genitive cow
And the unregarded shepherds
Alone dare gaze, unflinching,
At the tiny interrogative
— Why? — in the dirty straw.

CAROL

Brown is the earth: grey is the sky.
The pale straw glistens in frosty dusk.
The dry leaf curls and the bare boughs sigh.
The bright seed falls from the withered husk.
    The child of the world
        Lies curled
            Within this bed of straw.

Red is the berry and sharp the thorn,
But pale as the moon is the mistletoe fruit.
Tonight is the holy life reborn,
In blood and water the word takes root.
    The child of mind
        Lies curled
            Within this bed of straw.

Man and woman have come together.
Locked in their love is the human story.
The warmth of the heart defies the weather,
The gold of the straw dims Herod's glory.
    The child of love
        Lies curled
            Wihin this bed of straw.

PEASANT PHILOSOPHY

The little distant voices of the evening
Get lost under the huge impassive movement
Of continents of cloud, or the seamless blue
Of a retired disinterested sky.

Climatic armies taking up position
To launch tomorrow's weather, have no time
For the individual grief, the frightened child,
The just discovered lovers parted forever.

Anger, defiance, scorn or simple longing
Under historic night are the rabbit's scream,
The bull's incarcerated groan, the bird's whisper,
Each lonely creature moaning in his sleep.

Stay quiet, and exercise what love you may
To infiltrate the stirring soil, or knit
The roots of some few grasses. Do not look
For anything but anger from the sky.

THESE WERE THE DOVE DAYS

These were the dove-days
In the aspen-sequined garden
And the honey talk and the curious
Lizard streak of recognition,
With all the grass green with a natural pardon
For the spurious guilt, suspicion,
And the long-hardened
Arteries of a love deliberately
Denied, still known, now dazedly
Resurrected, when only the wasp-thrumming air
Can have been glitteringly aware
Of what Pandoran hasps
Had been furiously unfastened!

ASPEN, APPLE, ASH

Aspen, apple, ash, copper-beech, holm-oak,
Hawthorn, hornbeam, willow or wych-elm,
Sweet chestnut, rowan, cherry, or the smoke
Of olives on the terraced hillside — these
Shall clothe your spirit as seed in the haulme
From the Eden I have planted for you alone.

These are the integuments of natural pride:
Nothing to do with intricacies of guilt,
But burgeoning from a fine flesh on long-love's-bone–
Structure through despair indissolubly built:
Now on Cathedral columns in a green calm
A new love's forest flaunting its own leaves.

ONE DARK BIRD WANDERING

One dark bird wandering
Through a flat-glass-grey sky,
Dwindling, dwindling,
To invisibility;
And I
Stand at the open window
And cry

Like a spoiled child because
The world was not made
In the way
I would have planned,
And nothing I need
Or desire
Is close at hand.

Nor dare I require,
Or state
Or hope that it should be so:
Because in any case
It is now
Too late.

NOTES

p. 3   'Summer Beauty' was first published in the *London Mercury*, July 1936.
p. 5   'Return to Reality' was first published (as 'Poem') in the *London Mercury*, October 1936.
p. 7   'Elegy' was first published in *Twentieth Century Verse*, September 1937.
p. 8   'Fear' was first published in *Caravel*, March 1936.
p. 10 'Acres of Power' was first published in *New Writing*, Spring 1938; it was later reprinted in Maurice Carpenter, Jack Lindsay and Honor Arundel (eds), *New Lyrical Ballads* (1945) and in John Lehmann (ed), *Poems from New Writing 1936-46* (1946).
p. 12 'As Christmas Wanes' was first published in *New Writing*, Spring 1938.
p. 12 'The Prisoner' was first published in *Life and Letters Today*, Summer 1938, and in *New Lyrical Ballads*.
p. 14 'The Possible' was first published (as 'Poem') in *Left Review*, July 1936; it later appeared (as 'Comrade Heart') in *Poetry and the People*, July 1938 and (as 'The Possible') in both *Our Time*, December 1943, and *New Lyrical Ballads*.
p. 15 'Praise for the Anonymous' was first published in *Our Time*, July 1941.
p. 16 'After May Day' was first published in the *Daily Worker*, 13 May 1939, then in John Manifold (ed.), *The Book of Words* (1946); lines 24-26 were transposed in *The Years of Anger*, and are here restored to their original order as couplets.
p. 17 'Letter I' was first published in *Rhyme and Reason* (1944).
p. 21 'Letter V' was first published (as 'Poem') in *Life and Letters Today*, Winter 1937.
p. 22 'Letter VI' was first published (as 'Letter VII') in *Our Time*, August 1943 and in *New Lyrical Ballads*.
p. 22 'Letter VII' was first published (as 'Letter VIII') in *Rhyme and Reason* and in Oscar Williams (ed) *The War Poets* (1945).
p. 25 'Sussex in Winter' was first published in *Life and Letters Today*, November 1939 and Thomas Moult (ed), *The Best Poems of 1939*.
p. 29 In March 1939 Franco's armies entered Madrid and German troops entered Prague.
p. 44 'The Gothic Line' was first published in *Life and Letters Today*, September 1946 and in *The Book of Words*; 'Briefing for Invasion,' 'Between Agony and Desire' and 'The Day the War Ended' were first published in *Our Time*, February 1946.
p. 53 Sonnet 1 ('On the hither bank of battle'), Sonnet 2 ('Ah yes, he

will be captain of his soul'), Sonnet 3 ('Because he does not hope') and Sonnet 9 ('Glassy image of death') were first published in *Arena*, 1949; part of Sonnet 8 ('He hid his face') was published (as 'Man Without Love') in *Poetry Review*, January-February 1951.

p. 59 Alan Rawsthorne's setting of 'Incantation' and 'The Cave-artist's Prayer' was first performed in Edinburgh in 1967.

p. 65 'Song of the Hunger Marchers' was written with Alan Bush in early 1934 for the fifth national Hunger March; it was published later that year by the Workers Musical Association.

p. 66 'Before Morning' was published in *Left Review*, October 1934.

p. 66 'Man Like Sun' was published in *Poetry*, August 1935 and reprinted in Denys Kilham Roberts (ed.), *The Year's Poetry, 1935* (1935).

p. 67 'Especially When I Take Pen in Hand' was published (as 'Poem') in *Life and Letters Today*, Spring 1936, and in Thomas Moult (ed.), *The Best Poems of 1936* (1936).

p. 68 'Entrance to the City' is part of an unpublished 700 line poem written during 1934-5.

p. 69 'Spain' is the opening scene of Swingler's 'Mass Declamation' of the same title, first performed at Unity Theatre in November 1936 and subsequently all over Britain to raise money and support for the Spanish Republic.

p. 70 'They Live' was published in Nancy Cunard (ed), *Les Poetes du Monde Defend le Peuple Espagnol*, 6, 1937 and in David Martin (ed), *Rhyme and Reason* (1944); John Cornford and Ralph Fox were Communists killed defending democracy in Spain.

p. 71 'Friends, We Would Speak a Little of This Performance' is the text of the Chorale Finale of Alan Bush's Piano Concerto No. 1, first performed in 1938 on the BBC Home Service by the BBC Symphony Orchestra.

p. 74 'Triumphal Song for the Peacemaker' and 'After the Pogrom and the Stench of Blood' were evidently written after the Munich Agreement of September 1938; 'Triumphal Song for the Peacemaker' was published in *Poetry and the People*, November 1938; the 'Peacemaker' is the Tory Prime Minister, Neville Chamberlain.

p. 76 'Advance Democracy' was set to music by Benjamin Britten in 1938 and published by Boosey and Hawkes in 1939; a slightly different version of this poem appears in Boris Ford, ed., *Benjamin Britten's Poets*.

p. 77 'Ballad of Heroes', which also included verses by WH Auden from *On the Frontier*, was set to music by Benjamin Britten and first performed as part of the Festival of Music and the People at the Queen's Hall in April 1939, to mark the return of the last of the International Brigades to London.

p. 78 'On Some Who Were Killed Fighting in the International Brigade' appears to have been written in 1939; Swingler papers.

p. 80 'Make Your Meaning Clear' was written with Alan Bush and first performed at the Conway Hall in December 1939; Dimitrov was Secretary of the Comintern.

p. 81 'Sixty Cubic Feet' was first published in *Poetry and the People*, May 1940 and in *New Lyrical Ballads*; during the early months of the War it was frequently performed in London Underground shelters by Unity Theatre's Outside Show Group.

p. 82 'Drinking Song' was written and set to music by Christian Darnton in August 1941; it was published in *The Book of Words*.

p. 83 'Z Reserve' and 'Return to a Battlefield' appear in the notebooks which contain Swingler's other, published war poems.

p. 84 'Return to a Battlefield' was written sometime in late 1945 after Swingler returned to Monte Camino; like many Communists, Swingler was affectionately known in the Army as 'Joe' (after Marshall Stalin).

p. 86 'The Winter Journey' was first performed, with music by Alan Bush, at the Conway Hall in 1948.

p. 88 Swingler sent 'My Mistress Played' and 'To Geraldine' (over the name 'Randall Revividus') in a letter to Geraldine, 16 July 1949, whilst staying with Nancy Cunard at Lamothe-Fenelon; 'My Mistress Played' was set to music by John Sykes in the late 1950s.

p. 90 'Millie's Song' and 'Chorus' are from an opera, 'Fantasy Fair,' in Swingler's papers; he and Christian Darnton submitted the opera, unsuccessfully, to the Festival of Britain opera competition in 1949; 'Chorus' is taken from a longer song; the first verse is sung by the chorus, the second by Millie, the third by Steve; part of the opera was eventually performed at an Institute of Contemporary Arts concert of Darnton's work in 1953.

p. 91 'London Nocturne' was published in *Poetry Review*, October-November 1949.

p. 92 'Three Trees' was published in *Poetry Review*, September-October 1951; John Gawsworth was the editor of *Poetry Review*.

p. 92 'In the Labyrinth' was published in the Goldsmith's College students' poetry magazine, *Chapter and Verse*, September 1952.

p. 93 'The Ballad of Herod Templer' was written in 1952; General

NOTES TO PAGES 94-107   111

Templer had commanded the 56th Division during the Italian Winter campaign of 1943-4, prior to his role in suppressing the Communist insurgency in Malaya; in Swingler's papers.

p. 94   'Your Train Has Gone' was addressed to Christian Darnton after he left Britain for Italy in 1952 and was included in a letter from Swingler to Darnton, 26 March 1952.

p. 95   'The Harvest of Peace' was published in the *California Quarterly*, 1953; 'Korea' and 'The Soldier's Mother' were also published in *Daylight*, Autumn 1952; Bernard Stevens' setting of the sequence was first performed at the Conway Hall in 1953; a separate setting by Stevens of 'The Turning World' was performed in 1971.

p. 103   'A Rose for Lidice' was written for the 'Lidice Shall Live' campaign. Lidice was a small village in Czechoslovakia where all the men and most of the women and children were murdered during the War by the occupying German forces in reprisal for the assassination of Heydrich. Alan Rawsthorne's setting of the poem was first performed at the Arts Council in 1955 and then in the rebuilt village of Lidice in 1957.

p. 103   'The Fall of Babylon' was published in the *New Reasoner*, Autumn 1957.

p. 104   John Sykes' setting of 'Carol' was published in 1958 as *The Child of the World*.

p. 105   'Peasant Philosophy' was first published in the *Times Literary Supplement*, 19 May 1961.

p. 106   'These Were the Dove Days' is part of a long sequence entitled 'The Romantic's Adieu to Love' which Swingler wrote in 1966 to Penelope Mortimer; in Swingler's papers.

p. 106   Swingler sent 'Aspen, Apple, Ash' in a letter dated 10 October 19666 to his daughter, Deborah, to whom it is dedicated.

p. 107   'One Dark Bird Wandering' was written in 1967; this version is one of several in Swingler's papers.

ALSO FROM TRENT EDITIONS

Patrick Hamilton, *Impromptu in Moribundia*.
Price: £6.99 ISBN 0 905 488 33 4
Edited, with an introduction and notes, by Peter Widdowson, Professor of Literature at Cheltenham and Gloucester College of Higher Education.

H. G. Wells, *The Croquet Player*.
Price: £6.99 ISBN 0 905 48889 X
Edited, with an introduction and notes, by John Hammond, President of the H. G. Wells Society and a Research Fellow at The Nottingham Trent University.

Harriet E. Wilson, *Our Nig, or, Sketches from the Life of a Free Black*.
Price: £6.99 ISBN 0 905 48884 9
Edited, with an introduction and notes, by R J Ellis, Professor of English and American Studies at The Nottingham Trent University.

Henry James, *Hawthorne*.
Price: £6.99 ISBN 0 905488 43 1
Edited, with an introduction and notes, by Kate Fullbrook, Professor of Literary Studies at the University of the West of England.

Robert Bloomfield, *The Selected Poems of Robert Bloomfield*.
Price: £7.99 ISBN 0 905 48894 6
Edited by John Goodridge and John Lucas, with an Introduction by John Lucas. John Lucas is Research Professor of English, and John Goodridge is a Senior Lecturer in English, at The Nottingham Trent University.

George Garrett, *The Collected George Garrett*.
Price: £7.99 ISBN 0 905 488 48 2
Edited, with an introduction and notes, by Michael Murphy.
Michael Murphy's poems, essays, and reviews have appeared in *Critical Survey*, *London Magazine*, *Miscelania*, *Poetry Ireland Review* and *Symbiosis*. His first of collection poems, *After Attila*, is published by Shoestring Press. He is currently writing a thesis on Modern Poetry and Exile at The Nottingham Trent University.

ALSO FROM TRENT EDITIONS

William Barnes, *The Poems of William Barnes*.
Price: £7.99 ISBN 0 905 48895 4
Edited, with a critical commentary, by Valerie Shepherd, Reader in Linguistics at The Nottingham Trent University.

John Clare: *John Clare, The Living Year 1841*.
Price: £7.99 ISBN 0 905 488 55 5
Edited, with an introduction and notes, by Tim Chilcott, who has recently retired as Dean of the Faculty of Arts and Humanities at University College, Chichester.

Ronald Blythe, *Talking About John Clare*.
Price: £7.99 ISBN 0 905 488 44 X
Ronald Blythe is the President of the John Clare Society, and one of our most eminent rural writers. His famous account of a Suffolk village, *Akenfield*, has recently been re-issued by Penguin as a Twentieth Century Classic. His most recent publications are a book of essays, *Going to See George and Other Outings* (Long Barn Books, 1999); *First Friends* (Viking Penguin, 1999), a study of the young Paul and John Nash and Dora Carrington and their relationships in the period 1910-1920; and *Out of the Valley* (Viking Penguin, 2000), a journal in the style of *Word from Wormingford*.

Jim Burns, *Beats, Bohemians and Intellectuals*.
Price: £7.99 ISBN 0 905 488 57 1
Jim Burns is a widely published poet and critic. His most recent collections of poems are *Confessions of an Old Believer* (Redbeck Press, 1996) and *As Good a Reason As Any* (Redbeck Press, 1999).